Lao Tzu, author of Tao Te Ching

Return to Oneness with the Tao

Tao Te Ching Commentaries, Meditation and
Qigong for Healing and Spiritual Awakening

Ricardo B Serrano, Dipl.Ac.

Return to Oneness with the Tao

Tao Te Ching Commentaries, Meditation and
Qigong for Healing and Spiritual Awakening

Ricardo B Serrano, Dipl.Ac.

Published © Holisticwebs.com

ISBN 978-0-9877819-6-3

First published March 16, 2004
Published September 30, 2011
North Vancouver, B.C. Canada

FOREWORD

This book *Return to Oneness with the Tao* is my TCM master thesis on Taoist Yoga and other Meditation Models and was not solely written and published for commercial purposes, but rather, it is included as an essential supplementary material to the Qigong and meditation techniques and their effect, which is a combination of neurotransmitter changes, somatic effects, increased energy flow, relaxation-induced immune modulation, and psychoneuroimmunology, introduced in the *Meditation and Qigong Mastery, Return to Oneness with Spirit through Pan Gu Shen Gong* and *Six healing Qigong sounds with Mantras* books.

Cultivation of *Tao Healing Hands* is greatly assisted by the meditation and Qigong forms included in *Return to Oneness with the Tao* book and *Six healing Qigong sounds with Mantras* book. – Master Ricardo B Serrano

DISCLAIMER: The *Tao Healing Hands Compassion Blessings* are not a substitute for conventional medical diagnosis or treatment for any medical or psychological condition. Always consult your medical professional regarding any medical condition. There is no promise, guarantee or other warranty of any result.

An important fact that has to considered by holistic practitioners of meditation and Qigong is that every disease is the outcome of a specific *core emotional stress* or conflict that has to be identified and released to heal disease. When you go after the root cause of disease or "dis-ease" you open up possibilities of deep healing.

When you bring awareness to the emotional root cause – to the stress pattern and the associated thoughts and beliefs – you empower yourself to heal your life so you may heal physically. *We get sick because we are not aware. Awareness is the key to healing.*

According to Dr. Candace Pert, "When stress prevents the molecules of emotion from flowing freely where needed, the largely autonomic processes that are regulated by peptide flow, such as breathing, blood flow, immunity, digestion, and elimination, collapse down to a few simple feedback loop and upset the normal healing response. Meditation, by allowing long-buried thoughts and feelings to surface, is a way of getting the peptides flowing again, returning the body, and the emotions, to health."

Acknowledgement is given to Taoist Master Tao Huang and Edward Brennan for the use of their Tao Te Ching English translation. This book is dedicated in honor of Supreme Taoist Master Lao Jung Tzu with the hope to make his work known more to Lightworkers and benefit all the people around the world.

The author and Traditional Chinese Medicine practitioner Ricardo B Serrano has compiled his healing and transformation experiences with the meditation and Qigong forms as best as he can in his books for the benefit of readers. With thanks to Dr. Tao Grandmaster Zhi Gang Sha.

DISCLAIMER: This book is for educational and reference purposes only. Its contents are not intended as, nor are they a substitute for, personal one-on-one diagnosis or treatment by, or consultation with, a licensed health care practitioner.

Ricardo B Serrano will not be held liable for any adverse effects arising from the meditation practices. The physical and psychological conditions of each person vary. If adverse effects are experienced, stop the practice of the meditations immediately.

DEDICATIONS

To all the meditation and Qigong practitioners of every tradition.

"Understanding the laws and principles of the art and science of Meditation and Qigong is the first step in becoming its Master. "

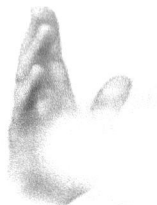

Tao Healing Hands
by
Master Ricardo B Serrano

You have the power to heal and transform yourself. - Master Ricardo B Serrano

As a culmination of his over 40 years of eastern spiritual studies, TCM and natural health research in cultivating self-healing, inner peace and rejuvenated energy, Master Ricardo B Serrano is proud to present Tao Healing Hands as an important vital adjunct to *Kuan Yin Lineage Holder* blessing. As Lao Tzu says, "To return to the Source is to find peace."

"Regular application of Tao Healing Hands healed my health challenges like fatigue, high blood pressure, failing left eyesight with soreness, and depression." – Ricardo B Serrano

Tao Healing Hands as a soul mind body healing approach can be applied in many situations, from everyday problems to serious chronic illness and mental and emotional distress. Tao Healing Hands is compatible with all other healing modalities and can enhance their effectiveness and has helped thousands of people to release stress and pain, to find happiness, and to discover new abilities and greater potential in their soul journey.

Read *Mantras for Shen Qi Jing channels*, page 7; *Tao Calligraphy*, page 57; *Tao Immortal Way Breathing*, page 68; *Mantra for Third Eye, page 86*; *Four spiritual channels*, page 92; *Soul Power* and *Tao Healing Hands,* page 88; *Six Healing Qigong sounds with Mantras by Master Ricardo B Serrano*

TABLE OF CONTENTS

Introduction . . . 6
Tao Ching . . . 9
Te Ching . . . 25
Epilogue . . . 47
Key Terms . . . 51
Commentary on I Ching (Book of Changes) . . . 54
Application of the Internal Alchemy (Neidan) of the Tao . . . 56
Tao Calligraphy & Song . . 57 The Internal Alchemy of the Tao . . 58
Cultivating Qi Energy in the Hara (Lower Dantian) . . . 65
Where Your Awareness (Attention) Goes, Energy Follows . . . 67
Tao Immortal Way Breathing . . . 68
Microcosmic Orbit Qigong . . . 69
Microcosmic Orbit Chart . . . 70
The Practice of the Microcosmic Orbit . . . 72
Important Notes . . . 73
Primordial Wuji Qigong for Enlightenment . . . 74
What is Tai Chi Mind in Tao Cosmology? . . . 75
Wuji Qigong as embodiment of Sacred Geometry . . . 76
What is Tai Chi for Enlightenment? . . . 78
Five Element Organ Correspondences . . . 80
Primordial Wuji Qigong Procedure . . . 82
Balancing Breathing Exercise . . . 85
The Caduceus . . . 86
Meditation on the Soul . . . 87
Warning . . . 88
What is Meditation on Twin Hearts? . . . 89
What Happens During the Meditation on Twin Hearts? . . . 90
Meditation on Twin Hearts Procedure . . . 91
Prayer of St. Francis of Assisi and Soul Song Love Peace and Harmony . . . 93
Why Practice Tibetan Shamanic Qigong (Qi Dao)? . . . 94
Addendum: Every Disease is the Outcome of Stress . . . 96
Whole Disease Approach with Wholistic View of Disease . . . 99
Quotations from book Molecules of Emotion . . . 100
Glossary . . . 101 TCM and sexual dysfunction . . . 102
Acknowledgements . . . 103
About Ricardo B Serrano . . . 104

INTRODUCTION

With great respect and love, I welcome you with all my heart. Lao Tzu's Tao TeChing has been my source of inspiration and guidance as a Way of the Tao since the early beginning of my Traditional Chinese Medicine studies and my path to self-realization and ascension. I would like to share with you part of my *TCM Master thesis on Taoist yoga and other meditation models* with this brief introduction regarding the importance of Te (virtue energy) cultivation in Lao Tzu's classic which is one of the most influential text in human history, and the single most important text in Chinese spirituality. The refinements obtained in the cultivation of Te in one's life and consciousness multiply the beneficial effects experienced in meditation at all levels.

Knowing the key terms used in the English translation of Tao Te Ching is the first step to enable a reader to understand the passages in the Tao Ching (The Classic Way) and the Te Ching (The Classic of Action /Integrity / Virtue) which are the two traditional divisions of Tao Te Ching (The Classic of the Way and Action to the Way).

I have chosen the English translation from the Mawangdui text by Edward Brennan and Tao Huang among the other excellent translations of this classic because I consider Tao Huang, a Taoist Master and Lao Tzu's channel medium, as my best choice among the other translators with his cultivation of (Te) virtue energy through neidan meditation practices, celestial contact with Lao Tzu himself and his additional comments regarding the I Ching (Book of Changes) which in turn can be demonstrated to have a direct relation to the human genetic code. He claims the unique distinction of having received direct inner spiritual initiation from Lao Tzu himself, and he is commissioned by him to teach Laoism in the West. He also shares the same belief as mine that cultivating Qi and Ching (sexual energy) through the Microcosmic Orbit and other Qigong practices should be integrated with Lao Tzu's Heart-sealed Teaching (similar to the Merkaba Light body activation) wherein he quoted, *"Sexuality is the base of everything, but mystic insight is the seed. This is the ultimate yin and yang, the harmony of body and mind."*

Although ascetics and hermits such as Shen Tao (who advocated that one 'abandon knowledge and discard self') first wrote of the 'Tao', it is with the sixth century B.C. philosopher Lao Jun Tzu (or 'Old Sage' -- born Li Erh) that the philosophy of Taoism really began. Some scholars believe that he was a slightly older contemporary of Confucius (Kung-Fu Tzu, born Chiu Chung-Ni). Other scholars feel that the Tao Te Ching, is really a compilation of paradoxical poems written by several Taoists using the pen-name, Lao Tzu. There is also a close association between Lao Tzu and the legendary Yellow Emperor, Huang-ti.

According to legend, Lao Tzu, Ascended Chinese Taoist Master and one of the Eight Immortals in the Taoist tradition, was keeper of the archives at the imperial court. When he was eighty years old he set out for the western border of China, toward what is now Tibet, saddened and disillusioned that men were unwilling to follow the path to natural goodness. At the border (Hank Pass), a guard, Yin Xi (Yin Hsi), asked Lao Tzu to record his teachings before he left. He then composed in 5,000 characters the Tao Te Ching (The Way and Its Power).

I have been contemplating the passages of this classic as part of my daily meditation practices. I find from my experience that they are also a means - through the encoded energy vibration within the poetic words and Lao Tzu's voice - to induce a meditative superconscious state enabling the reader to contact Ascended Master Lao Tzu's wisdom and the light and love of the Tao or Spirit during regular contemplation of the passages.

May you benefit greatly from practicing the neidan (inner alchemy) meditation and contemplating regularly the classic's passages which are full of gems of wisdom for living a life of peace, love, and enlightenment as an ascended being or a lightworker on the path with beloved Master Lao Tzu as your Spirit Master guide and companion. If you have questions about the materials in Tao Te Ching, **go directly and ask Master Lao Tzu. You must strive to connect directly to Master Lao Tzu's original mind and the energetic vibration generated through Lao Tzu. You need a direct spiritual sensation passed down by Master Lao Tzu.**

Updated from my book Six healing Qigong sounds with Mantras (2021): *Mantras to clear blockages in Shen Qi Jing channels are necessary to heal all sickness, attain rejuvenation and longevity, and to reach Tao (immortality). Da Bei Zhou compassion mantra is also necessary to heal all sickness and attain supreme enlightenment.*

I am happy to say that the three years of study in the Tao Academy on Soul Healing that includes Da Bei Zhou chanting, Tao Healing Hands and Soul Communication have, I believe, completed my Chinese medicine studies including Tai Chi and Qigong under the tutelage of Tai Chi and Qigong Lineage holders. I have also updated this book *Return to Oneness with the Tao* to include what I have learned and experienced from my studies with the Tao Academy under the tutelage of certified Tao Academy Master Teachers (2021 – 2023).

Soul Healing is not similar to Qigong healing. Qigong is energy healing. We go beyond energy. It's Divine Healing Hands or Divine Soul Healing. We can do one-to-one healing, group healing, and distance healing. There are all kinds of sickness in the physical, emotional, mental, and spiritual bodies. To heal and transform humanity, we must remove Jing qi shen blockages. Jing qi shen blockages are the biggest pollution.

How do we fix this or purify the blockages? I learned the Five Power Techniques to purify Jing qi shen. They are Body Power, Soul Power, Mind Power, Sound Power, and Tao Calligraphy Power. Body Power means that when you meditate, you use special hand and body position, like a mudra, for healing and purification. Soul Power is to say hello. You say hello to the inner souls of your systems, organs, cells, or parts of the body. You also say hello to outer souls, including Heaven, Mother Earth, the Divine, Tao, and all kinds of saints. Mind Power is to visualize light. Simply visualizing golden and rainbow light is a vital technique. Sound Power is to chant healing mantras for healing and purification. Tao Calligraphy Power is to apply the healing calligraphies that Master Sha wrote where he asked the Source to transfer Source Jing qi shen to the calligraphies.

I would like to personally thank Master Tao Huang for his permission to use his Tao TeChing English translation in this book, and also thank and acknowledge Universal Tao's Master Tao Huang and Master Mantak Chia, authors of *Door to All Wonders* which *I highly recommend you read for a complete theoretical and technical rundown on the application of the chapters and verses in Tao Te Ching*; Edward Brennan, a translator of Tao Te Ching; David Hinton, translator of Tao Te Ching, Lao Tzu; and most of all, ascended Master Lao Tzu and the lineage of the Tao Immortals, for their great contribution in the writing of this short book.

I would also like to acknowledge and thank especially Michael Winn, my American Taoist sage teacher at Healing Tao USA, for his teachings which greatly developed my understanding of the Taoist fusion of the five elements, inner smile, healing love, Kan and Li internal alchemy and Primordial Qigong: Tai Chi for Enlightenment.

I would also like to acknowledge and thank my Arhat and Pranic Healing teacher Grand Master Choa Kok Sui for his Meditation on Twin Hearts and Meditation on the Soul.
Caution: Do not practice Shen Gong meditations such as Meditation on Twin Hearts and Meditation on the Soul without first training the Lower Dantian to root to avoid self induced energetic psychosis.

I would like to acknowledge and thank Lama Tantrapa, my Tibetan Shamanic Qigong teacher, for teaching me Qi Dao, Dr. Candace Pert for Quotations from her inspiring book *Molecules of Emotion,* and Dr. Nelie Johnson, MD from Maple Ridge, B.C. for her inspiring article *You Hold the Keys to Your Healing* which supports my research and experience that there is a stress energy profile in the background of all illness and disease, and that you heal disease when you clear the cause by identifying and releasing the associated pattern of stress. The body can heal itself when there is no emotional block in the way, including your own fears.

Quotations from Dr. Bruce Lipton, Dr. Claude Sabbah and Dr. Candace Pert on the Wholistic View of Disease are included toward an expanded model of disease and patient empowerment.

"True Qi is the prenatal Qi from the parents, Qi of the breathing from Heaven and Qi of food and water from Earth, mixing together." - Ling Shu

Buteyko Breathing is the first strategy I use before and during meditation and exercise to achieve optimal healing in my physical, mental and spiritual bodies. - *Ricardo B Serrano, Dipl.Ac.,* Read *Buteyko Method, p. 85* With thanks to Buteyko breathing teacher Patrick McKeown, author of *The Breathing Cure* book.

With thanks to *Tai Chi Master Helen Liang*, whose 13-posture Tai Chi movements promote Qi flow.

When you're "going with the flow," or in a state of *Wu Wei* via the 13-posture Tai Chi, supple as water, strong as the mountain, you maintain inner tranquility in your everyday life by promoting smooth flow of Qi and blood, and *embody being in the flow*. Read *13-postures Tai Chi by Master Helen Liang,* page 95

Lastly, with thanks and acknowledgement to *Master Zhi Gang Sha*, whose *Da Bei Zhou* and *Tao Hands* teachings brought my search to oneness with the Tao to a fruitful end.

Soul healing is a simple, fast way to cure your negative emotions. – Ricardo B Serrano, Soul Healer
Opening your heart to the unconditional love of the universe (Tao Source) is the way. – *Lao Tzu*, read page 56

In the One Heart of the One Love, Ricardo B. Serrano, R.Ac., Tao Hands Practitioner

"The teaching focuses essentially on the purification of Jing-Chi-Shen into its final product: the elixir of pure-person."
- Door to All Wonders

TAO TE CHING (The Classic Way) **Translated by Edward Brennan and Tao Huang**

I. Tao Ching (The Classic of Way)

Chapter 1

1. Tao that is voiced is no longer that of eternal Tao.
   The name that has been written is no longer that of eternal name.

2. The nameless is the beginning of the cosmic universe.
   The named is the mother of the myriad creatures.

3. Being at peace, one can see into the subtle.
   Engaging with passion, one can see into the manifest.

4. They both arise from a common source but have different names.
   Both are called the mystery within the mystery.
   They are the door to all wonders.

Chapter 2

1. In the world,
   Everyone recognizes beauty as beauty,
   Since the ugly is also there.
   Everyone recognizes goodness as goodness,
   Since evil is also there.

2. Since Being and non-being give birth to each other,
   Difficulty and ease complete each other,
   Long and short measure each other,
   High and low overflow into each other,
   Voice and sound harmonize with each other,
   And before and after follow each other.

3. Therefore the sage
   Lives in action less engagement,
   And preaches wordless doctrine.

4. The myriad creatures
   Act without beginning,
   Nourish without possessing,
   Accomplish without claiming credit.

5. It is accomplishment without claiming credit
   that makes the outcome self-sustaining.

Chapter 3

1. Do not exalt intelligence and people will not compete;
   Do not value rare goods and people will not steal;
   Do not display for public view and people will not desire.

2. So the sage's governing methods are:
   Emptying the mind, Vitalizing the stomach,
   Softening the will, Strengthening the character.

3. This always makes people not know and not desire.
   This always makes the knower dare not act.
   Therefore, nothing is beyond ruling.

Chapter 4

1. Tao functions in itself empty harmony.
   When used, it remains full.

2. For sure, this source is the very ancestor of the myriad things.

3. Blunting the sharp edges,
   Un-ravelling the tangles,
   Husbanding into the light,
   Being as ordinary as the dust.

4. Ah! Limpid, it seems to exist forever

5. Ah! Limpid, it seems to exist forever

Chapter 5

1. Nature has no benevolence,
   It treats all things like straw-dogs;
   The sage has no benevolence,
   He treats his people like straw-dogs.

2. Between heaven and earth it seems like a bellow:
   Empty, yet inexhaustible,
   The stronger it is activated, the greater the output.

3. Being overly informed leads to exhaustion,
   Better to be centered.

Chapter 6

1. Valley-spirit is deathless, It is called the mystical female.
2. The gateway of the mystical female, is called the root of heaven and earth.
3. Hovering, it seems ever-present. Put to use, it is never exhausted.

Chapter 7

1. Heaven is eternal, and earth is long-lasting.
2. What makes heaven and earth eternal and long-lasting
   is that they do not give birth to themselves.
   It is this that makes them eternal and long-lasting.

3. Hence the sage,
   Relaxing the body, the body comes to the fore.
   Beyond the body, the body comes to the fore.
   Beyond the body, the body exists of itself.

4. Not even relying on selflessness, enables the self to be fulfilled.

Chapter 8

1. Eminent goodness is like water.
2. Water is good at benefitting all things,
   Yet it actively competes.
   It retires to undesirable places.
   Thus it is near to Tao.

3. Dwelling in good places,
   Drawing from good sources,
   Supplying from good nature,
   Speaking with good trust,
   Governing with good rules,
   Conducting with good ability,
   And acting within good time.

4. For this reason,
   There is no competition,
   There is no concern.

Chapter 9

1. Hanging on to it will cause overflow; better to let go.
   Forced consent does not endure.
   Filling the house with gold and jade will not bring safety.
   Riches and royalty result in pride; they bring about their own punishment.

2. When the work is done, the body withdraws.
   This is the Tao of heaven.

Chapter 10

1. Donning the spirit and soul, and drawing them into Oneness,
   Can this come apart?
   Gathering in Chi and making the body supple, is this not an infant?
   Being clear-headed and eliminating any mystic vision,
   Can even a speck exist?
   Loving the people and governing the country,
   Is this not inactive?
   Opening and closing the Gate of Heaven,
   Is this not the female?
   Comprehending the four corners of the world,
   Is this not knowledge?

2. Begetting and nourishing;
   Begetting but not possessing,
   Enhancing but not dominating.

3. This is Mysterious Action.

Chapter 11

1. Thirty spokes join at one hub,
   Yet it is the emptiness inside the hub that makes the vehicle useful;
   Clay is molded into a vessel,
   Yet it is the hollowness that makes the vessel useful;
   Windows and doors are cut out,
   Yet it is their empty space that makes the room usable.

2. So, any having makes for excess,
   Any not-having makes for usefulness.

Chapter 12

1. Five colors blind the eyes.
   Racing and hunting madden the heart.
   Pursuing what is rare makes action deceitful.
   Five flavors dull the palate.
   Five tones deafen the ears.

2. So, the sage's method is for the belly, not for the eyes.
   He abandons the latter and chooses the former.

Chapter 13

1. Favor and disgrace surprise the most.
   Value the trouble as you do the body.

2. Why do "favor and disgrace surprise the most"?
   Favor enhances only the inferior,
   Receiving it is a surprise,
   And losing it is also a surprise.
   This is why "favor and disgrace surprise the most".

3. Why to "value the trouble as you do the body"?
   It is only because I have a body that I have trouble.
   If I did not have a body, where would the trouble be?

4. So, if you value the world as you do the body,
   You can be entrusted with the world;
   If you love the body as you love the beauty of the world,
   You can be responsible for the world.

Chapter 14

1. Look for it and not to be seen, it is called invisible;
   Listen to it and not to be heard, it is called inaudible;
   Reach for it and not to be touched, it is called intangible.

2. These three are beyond reckoning, so
   When these three merge, they are One.

3. As for this One, there is nothing above it remaining to be accounted for,
   There is nothing below it that has been excluded.
   Ever searching for it, it is beyond naming.

4. It returns to no-thing.
   Its state is described as no state,
   Its form is described as formless.
   It is called the vision beyond focus.

5. Follow after it, and it proves endless.
   Go before it, and no beginning can be found.

6. Employ the Tao of today in order to manage today's affairs
   and to know the ancient past.

7. This is called the principle of Tao.

Chapter 15

1. The ancient sages of Tao are subtle and mysteriously penetrating. Their depth is beyond the power of will.

2. Because it is beyond the power of will, The
   most we can do is describe it:

3. Thus, Full of care, as one crossing the wintry stream, Attentive,
   as one cautious of the total environment, Reserved, as one
   who is a guest,
   Spread open, as when confronting a marsh, Simple,
   like uncarved wood, Opaque, like mud, Magnificent,
   like a valley.

4. From within the murky comes the stillness. The
   feminine enlivens with her milk.

5. Keeping such a Tao, excess is undesirable.
   Desiring no excess, work is completed without exhaustion.

Chapter 16

1. Reaching the ultimate emptiness,
   Concentrating on the central stillness,
   All things work together.

2. From this I observe their returning.
3. All things under heaven flourish in their vitality,
   Yet each returns to its own root.
   This is stillness.
   Stillness means returning to its destiny.
   Returning to its destiny is steadfastness.
   To know steadfastness means enlightenment.
   Not to know steadfastness is to act forcefully.
   Acting forcefully brings disaster.
   Knowing the steadfast implies acceptance.
   Acceptance is impartial.
   Impartial is regal. Regal is heaven. Heaven is Tao.
   Tao is beyond danger even when the body perishes.

Chapter 17

1. The eminent has consciousness of self.
   The next down are loved and praised.
   The next down are feared,
   At the bottom is the source.

2. When faith is weak, there is distrust.
   Especially in the worth of speech.

3. Results speak for themselves.
   This, people call me Nature.

Chapter 18

1. When the Great Tao is abandoned,
   There is benevolence and righteousness.
   When intelligence arises,
   There is a great deal of manipulation.
   When there is disharmony in the family,
   There comes about filial piety.
   When the country is in big trouble,
   There arises patriotism.

Chapter 19

1. Get rid of wisdom, abandon intelligence, and
   People will benefit a hundredfold.
   Get rid of benevolence, abandon justice, and
   People will return to filial piety and kindness.
   Get rid of skill, abandon profit, and
   Thieves will disappear.

2. These three are inadequate.
   So just let things be.

3. Observe the plain and embrace the simple.
   Do not think much and do not desire much,
   Get rid of learning and worry will disappear.

Chapter 20

1. How much difference is there between yea and nay?
   How much difference is there between beautiful and ugly?

2. What one fears is what he cannot help but fear.
3. One is in the wilderness without central ground.
4. Ordinary people are fulfilled,
   Eating delicious food,
   Reaching the climax of romance.
   I am desire less and without anticipation,
   Like a baby who does not yet.
   Gathering energy together, entering the abyss beyond the point of no return.

5. Ordinary people have more than enough,
   I am a fool at heart, as a water droplet is to the spring.

6. People of affairs are bright and intelligent.
   I alone am unintelligent.
   People of affairs are cunning and clever.
   I alone am dull and unsophisticated,
   Unnoticed in the depth of the sea,
   Looked for in an endless horizon.

7. Ordinary people are productive,
   I alone maintain the living essence within.
   I alone stay with a unitary source, as if stubborn.

8. I want to be wholly different from everyone else,
   By taking my sustenance from the mother source.

Chapter 21

1. The marks of profound action follow only from the Tao.
2. The substance of Tao is boundless and unfathomable.
   Unfathomable and boundless,
   In its center there is form;
   Boundless and unfathomable,
   In its center there is an object;
   Embryonic and dark,
   In its center there is essence;
   The essence is very pure,
   In its center there is trust.
   From now to the days of old,
   Its name never dies,
   Because it creates all things in their beginning.

3. How do I know the source of all beginnings?
   From this.

Chapter 22

1. Those who boast of themselves lose their stance.
   He who displays himself is not seen.
   He who justifies himself is not understood.
   He who lashes out does not succeed.
   He who builds himself up does not endure.

2. In the sense of Tao,
   This is said to be eating too much and acting too much.
   It results in disgust.

3. Those who desire will not endure.

Chapter 23

1. Yield, and retain integrity.
   In the depths of whirling, there is stillness.
   The hollow enables the plentiful.
   The old gives way to the new.
   The small allows for increase.
   Excess breeds confusion.

2. Therefore the sage holds oneness as the shepherd of the world.
3. He who does not display himself is seen.
   He who does not justify himself is understood.
   He who does not lash out succeeds.
   He who does not build himself up endures.

4. Therefore, only the spirit of non-competition makes things non-competitive.
5. So the old saying, "yield, and retain integrity," is but a few words.
   But when rightly understood, integrity returns.

Chapter 24

1. Natural speech consists of few words.
2. Gusty winds do not last all morning,
   Cloudbursts do not last all day.
   What makes this so?

3. Heaven and earth will not last forever,
   How could a human being last!

4. So the person who works according to Tao unites with Tao.
   In the same way he unites with action.
   In the same way he unites with loss.

5. Uniting with action, the Tao becomes action.
   Uniting with loss, the Tao becomes loss.

Chapter 25

1. Matter is formed from chaos.
   It was born before heaven and earth.
   Silent and void.
   Standing alone, without territory,
   Able to be mother to the world.

2. I do not yet know its name,
   I call it Tao.
   With reluctance I deem it to be Great.
   Great refers to the symbol.
   The symbol refers to what is remote.
   What is remote refers to returning.

3. Tao is great.
   Heaven is great.
   Earth is great.
   Kingship is great.
   These are the four great things in the world,
   Kingship is one of them.

4. Humankind takes its origin from earth.
   Earth takes her origin from heaven.
   Heaven takes its origin from Tao.
   Tao takes its origin from Nature.

Chapter 26

1. The heavy is the root of the light.
   Tranquility is the master of the restless.

2. Thus, the noble person will travel all day without leaving his seat.
   Though the center of the highest authority,
   And surrounded by luxury,
   He remains clear minded.

3. How could the king of myriad chariots treat his body
   with less care than he gives the country?

4. Being careless loses the foundation.
   Being restless loses mastery.

Chapter 27

1. A good traveler leaves no tracks.
   A good speaker is without flaw.
   A good planner does not calculate.
   A good doorkeeper does not lock, yet it cannot be opened.
   A good knot maker does not use binding, yet it cannot be undone.

2. Therefore, the sage is good at his earnest demands upon people.
   So no one is left out.
   No talent is wasted.
   This is called being in the tow of enlightenment,
   And it ensures the good person.

3. For everything that is good is the teacher of the good person.
   Everything that is bad becomes a resource for the good person.
   No need to honor the teachers.
   No need to love the resources.

4. Though knowing this is a great paradox,
   It is the subtle principle.

Chapter 28

1. Understanding the male and holding onto the female
   Enables the flow of the world.
   This being the flow of the world, the eternal action abides.
   Knowing that the eternal action abides is to return to childhood.

2. Understanding the pure and holding on to the impure
   Enables the cleansing of the world.
   With the cleansing of the world, ongoing action suffices.
   When ongoing action suffices, it returns to simplicity.

3. Understanding the white and holding on to the black
   Enables the formation of the world.
   Being the formation of the world, ongoing action does not stray.
   When ongoing action does not stray, it returns to the infinite.

4. This simplicity takes shape as a mechanism.
   The sage makes it the head ruler.
   Great ruling never divides.

Chapter 29

1. I see that those who want to take over the world
   and manipulate it do not succeed.

2. The sacred mechanism of the world cannot be manipulated.
   Those who manipulate it will fail,
   Those who hold on to it will lose it.

3. Matter
   Either leads or follows,
   Either heats or chills,
   Either strengthens or weakens,
   Either enhances or destroys.

4. So the sage abandons extremes, extravagance, multiplicity.

Chapter 30

1. Using the Tao as the rule for governing the people,
   Do not employ the army as the power of the world.
   For this is likely to backfire.

2. Where the army has marched, thorns and briars grow.
3. Being good has its own consequence,
   Which cannot be seized by power.

4. Achieving without arrogance,
   Achieving without bragging,
   Achieving without damage,
   Achieving without taking ownership.
   This is called achieving without force.

5. Matter becomes strong, then old.
   This is called "Not-Tao".
   Dying young is "Not-Tao".

Chapter 31

1. The army is the mechanism of bad luck.
   The elements of the world may oppose.
   So those who have ambitions cannot rest.

2. Therefore the nobleman takes his
   place on the left side,
   And the commander on the right side.

3. So the army is not the nobleman's weapon.
   As a mechanism of bad luck,
   He uses it only as the last resort.
   Then the best way is to use it quickly and destructively.
   Do not enjoy this.
   To take delight in it is to enjoy killing people.
   Those who enjoy killing people do not attract the favor of the world.

4. The good inclines to the left,
   The bad inclines to the right.

5. Thus the intelligent officer stays on the left,
   The army commander stays on the right.

6. Speaking in an image of sadness,
   After killing the people, every one stands in mourning.
   Victory is celebrated as a funeral service.

Chapter 32

1. Tao is eternally nameless.
2. Though simplicity is small,
   The world cannot treat it as subservient.
   If lords and rulers can hold on to it,
   Everything becomes self-sufficient.

3. Heaven and earth combine and allow sweet dew.
   Without rules, people will naturally become equal.

4. At the outset, the rule must be expressed.
   Once it exists, stop speaking of it.
   The result of not speaking of it is to eliminate danger.

5. In a manner of speaking, Tao is to the world
   As the rivers are to oceans and seas.

Chapter 33

1. To know others is to be knowledgeable,
   To know oneself is enlightenment;
   To master others is to have strength,
   To master oneself is to be powerful.

2. To know what is sufficient is to be rich.
   To act with determination is to have will.
   Not to lose one's substance is to endure.
   To die, but not be forgotten, is to be immortal.

Chapter 34

1. As the Tao is all-pervading,
   It operates on both the left and the right.

2. Success is consequent to all affairs.
   It does not proclaim its own existence.
   All things return.
   Yet there is no claim of ownership,
   So it is forever desires.
   This can be called small.
   All things return.
   Yet there is no claim of ownership,
   This can be called great.

3. The sage accomplishes greatness in not acting great.
   Thus can he accomplish what is great.

Chapter 35

1. Holding on to the great Symbol,
   The whole world carries on.
   On and on without doing harm.

2. Being happy at peace,
   Enjoying greatly the music and food.
   Travelers stop by.

3. When the Tao is spoken forth plainly
   It has no flavor at all.

4. Look, but that is not sufficient for seeing.
   Listen, but that is not sufficient for hearing.
   Use it, but it is not exhausted.

Chapter 36

1. When you want to constrict something,
   You must first let it expand;
   When you want to weaken something,
   You must first enable it;
   When you want to eliminate something,
   You must first allow it;
   When you want to conquer something,
   You must first let it be.
   This is called the Fine Light.

2. The weak overcomes the strong.
   Fish cannot live away from the source.
   The sharp weapon of the nation should never be displayed.

Chapter 37

1. Tao is eternally nameless.
   If lords and rulers would abide by it,
   All things would evolve of themselves.

2. What evolves desires to act.
   I, then, suffuse this with nameless simplicity.
   Suffusing with nameless simplicity is eliminating humiliation.
   Without humiliation, peace arises.
   Heaven and earth regulate themselves.

(above Tao Te Ching passages courtesy of Universal tao)

Translated by Edward Brennan and Tao Huang

II. Te Ching (The Classic of Action / Integrity / Virtue)

Chapter 38

1. Eminent action is inaction,
   For that action it is active.
   Inferior action never stops acting,
   For that reason it is inactive.

2. Eminent action is disengaged,
   Yet nothing is left unfulfilled;
   Eminent humanness engages,
   Yet nothing is left unfulfilled;
   When eminent righteousness engages,
   It reduces the results of engagements;
   Eminent justice engages, but does not respond adequately to situations.
   For that reason it is frustrated.

3. When Tao is lost,
   It becomes Action;
   When Action is lost,
   It becomes benevolence;
   When benevolence is lost,
   It becomes justice.
   When justice is lost,
   It becomes propriety.

4. Propriety is the veneer of faith and loyalty,
   And the forefront of troubles.

5. Foresight is the vain display of Tao,
   And the forefront of foolishness.

6. Therefore, the man of substance
   Dwells in wholeness rather than veneer,
   Dwells in the essence rather than the vain display.

7. He rejects the latter, and accepts the former.

Chapter 39

1. Those from the past have attained Oneness.
2. By attaining Oneness, heaven is clear.
   By attaining Oneness, earth is at peace.
   By attaining Oneness, the spirit is quickened.
   By attaining Oneness, the valley is filled.
   By attaining Oneness, the king puts order in the whole world.
   All these result from Oneness.

3. Without its clarity, heaven is liable to explode.
   Without its peace, earth is liable to erupt.
   Without its quickening, the spirit is liable to die out.
   Without its fullness, valleys are liable to dry out.
   Without proper esteem, the king is liable to fall.

4. Esteem is rooted in the humble.
   The high is founded upon the low.

5. This is why the lords and rulers call themselves widows and orphans without support.
   Is this is not the root of being humble?

6. Much praise amounts to no praise.
7. Without preference, Being is as resonant as Jade and as gravelly as stone.

Chapter 40

1. When eminent persons hear of Tao,
   They practice it faithfully;
   When average persons hear of Tao,
   It seems that they practice it, and it seems they do not;
   When inferior persons hear of Tao,
   They ridicule it.

2. Without such ridicule, it would not be Tao.

3. Thus, the aphorism that suggests the way is:
   Knowing the Tao seems costly.
   Entering Tao seems like retreating.
   Becoming equal with Tao gives birth to paradoxes.
   Eminent action is like a valley.
   Complete understanding resembles being disgraced.
   Vast action seems yielding.
   Action that builds up seems remiss.
   Pure integrity seems perverse.
   The great square has no angles.
   The great talent matures late.
   The great voice sounds faint.
   The great image has no form.
   The Tao is praised but is un-nameable.

4. Only Tao is good at beginning and good at completion.

Chapter 41

1. Tao moves by returning.
   Tao functions by weakness.

2. All things under heaven are born of being.
   Being is born of non-being.

Chapter 42

1. Tao gives rise to one.
    One gives rise to two.
    Two gives rise to three.
    Three gives rise to all things.

2. All things carry yin and embrace yang.
    Drawing chi together into harmony.

3. What the world hates is the widow and orphan without support.
    But lords and rulers name themselves these.

4. Do not seek gain from losing, nor loss from gaining.
5. What people teach, after discussion becomes doctrine.
6. Those who excel in strength do not prevail over death.
    I would use this as the father of teaching.

Chapter 43

1. What is softest in the world penetrates what is hardest in the world.
    Non-being enters where there is no room.

2. From this I know the riches of non-action.
3. Wordless teaching and the riches of non-action is matched by very little in the world.

Chapter 44

1. Which is more cherished, the name or the body?
    Which is worth more, the body or possessions?
    Which is more beneficial, to gain or to lose?

2. Extreme fondness is necessarily very costly.
    The more you cling to, the more you lose.

3. So knowing what is sufficient averts disgrace.
    Knowing when to stop averts danger.
    This can lead to a longer life.

Chapter 45

1. Grand perfection seems lacking, yet its use is never exhausted.
   Grand fullness seems empty, yet its use never comes to an end.
   Grand straightforwardness seems bent.
   Grand skill seems clumsy.
   Grand surplus seems deficient.

2. Activity overcomes cold.
   Stillness overcomes heat.
   Peace and tranquility can be the measure of the world.

Chapter 46

1. When there is Tao in the world, work horses are used to fertilize the land.
   Without Tao in the world, the war horse flourishes in the countryside.

2. There is no crime greater than fostering desire.
   There is no disaster greater than not knowing when there is enough.
   There is no fault greater than wanting to possess.

3. Knowing that sufficiency is enough always suffices.

Chapter 47

1. In order to know the world, do not step outside the door.
   In order to know the Tao of heaven, do not peer through the window.

2. The further out you go, the less you know.
3. So the sage knows without moving, identifies without seeing, accomplishes without acting.

Chapter 48

1. Having a zest for learning yields an increase day by day.
   Hearing the Tao brings a loss day by day.
   Losing more and more until inaction results.
   Inaction results, yet everything is done.

2. Managing the world always involves non-engagement.
   As soon as there is engagement, there is never enough of it to manage the world.

Chapter 49

1. The sage is always without his own mind.
   He uses people's minds as his mind.

2. He is kind to those who are kind.
   He is also kind to those who are not kind.
   It is the kindness of Action itself.
   He is trustworthy to those who are trustworthy.
   He is also trustworthy to those who are not trustworthy.
   It is the trust of Action itself.

3. In the world, the sage inhales.
   For the world, the sage keeps the mind simple.

4. All people are fixated on the ears and eyes.
   While the sage always smiles like a child.

Chapter 50

1. We live, we die.

2. The companions of life are three and ten.
   The companions of death are three and ten.
   That people live their active life necessarily
   leading to the ground of death is three and ten.

3. Why so? it is the nature of life itself.

4. As a matter of fact, I hear of those who are good at preserving their lives;
   Walking through, not avoiding rhinos and tigers.
   Entering battle without wearing armaments.
   The rhino has no place to dig its horns.
   The tiger has no place to drag its claws.
   The soldier has no place to thrust his blade.

5. Why is this so?
   Because they have no place to die.

Chapter 51

1. Tao enlivens.
   Action nourishes.
   Matter forms.
   Mechanism completes.
   For that reason, all things worship Tao and exalt Action.

2. The worship of Tao and exaltation of Action are not conferred,
   but always arise naturally.

3. Tao enlivens and nourishes, develops and cultivates,
   integrates and completes, raises and sustains.

4. It enlivens without possessing.
   It acts without relying.
   It develops without controlling.

5. Such is called mystic Action.

Chapter 52

1. The world begins with the mother as its source.
2. When you have the mother, you know the son.
   When you know the son, return to preserve the mother.
   Although the body dies, there is no harm.

3. By closing your mouth and shutting the door,
   there would be no wearing down of life.
   When opening the mouth and pursuing your affairs, life cannot be preserved.

4. Seeing what is small is discernment.
   Preserving subtleness is strength.
   Using the light enables one to return to discernment.

5. Without losing the center of the body is called penetrating the eternal.

Chapter 53

1. Through discrimination, I have the knowledge to walk in the great Tao.
   The only fear is what is other than that.

2. The great Tao is quite smooth, yet people prefer a short-cut.
   The court is so busy legislating that the fields go uncultivated
   and granaries are all empty.
   They wear the magnificent clothing, girdle the sharp swords.
   They are gorged with food and possess many brides.
   Their bounty suffices but they continue to steal.

3. This is opposite of Tao.

Chapter 54

1. What is well-built is not pulled down.
   What is well-fastened is not separated.
   Sons and grandsons worship unceasingly.

2. Cultivate the self, and the Action is pure.
   Cultivate the family, the Action is plentiful.
   Cultivate the community, the Action endures.
   Cultivate the nation, the Action is fruitful.
   Cultivate the world, the Action is all-pervading.

3. Treat the self by the standard of self.
   Treat the family by the standard of family.
   Treat the community by the standard of community.
   Treat the nation by the standard of nation.
   Treat the world by the standard of world.

4. How do I know how the world is such?
   Thus.

Chapter 55

1. Action in its profundity is like a newborn baby.
   Poisonous insects and venomous snakes do not sting it.
   Predatory birds and ferocious animals do not seize it.

2. Its bones are soft and its sinews supple, yet its grasp is firm;
   Without knowing the union of male and female, its organs become aroused.
   Its vital essence comes to the point;
   Crying all day, its voice never becomes hoarse.
   Its harmony comes to the point.

3. Harmony is eternal.
   Knowing harmony is discernment.
   Enhancing life is equanimity.
   Generating vitality through mind is strength.

4. When things reach their climax, they are suddenly old.
5. This is "Non-Tao".
   "Non-Tao" dies young.

Chapter 56

1. Those who know, do not say.
   Those who say, do not know.

2. Close the mouth.
   Shut the door.
   Merge into light.
   As ordinary as dust.
   Blunt the sharpness.
   Unravel the entanglements.

3. This is called mysterious sameness.

4. You are not intimate by acquiring it.
   You are not distant in not acquiring it;
   You do not profiting by acquiring it.
   You do not lose it by not acquiring it;
   You are not ennobled by acquiring it.
   You are not disgraced by not acquiring it.

5. This enables the nobility of the world.

Chapter 57

1. Using the right lawfulness to govern the country.
   Using un-expectancy to conduct the battle.
   Using disengagement to take over the world.

2. How do I know this is so?
   Thus.

3. The more prohibitions there are in the world, the poorer people will be.
   The more destructive weapons people have, the more chaotic the nation will become.
   The more know-how people have, the more bizarre things will appear.
   The more rules and demands that flourish, the more thefts there will be.

4. Therefore the sage says:
   When I am inactive, people transform themselves.
   When I abide in stillness, people organize themselves lawfully.
   When I am disengaged, people enrich themselves.
   When I choose non-desire, people remain simple.

Chapter 58

1. When the government is silent, people are sincere.
   When the government is intrusive, the state is decisive.

2. Disaster is what fortune depends upon,
   Fortune is what disaster subdues.
   Who knows a final outcome?

3. There is no right lawfulness.
   Justice tends towards the extreme.
   Kindness tends towards evil.
   People have been familiar with this for a long time.

4. So,
   Be rounded without cutting.
   Be compatible without puncturing.
   Be straightforward without trapping.
   Be bright without dazzling.

Chapter 59

1. For governing people and serving the heaven,
   nothing is better than frugality.

2. Only frugality enables the pre-empty measures.
   Pre-empty measures mean a great accumulation of Action.
   A great accumulation of Action leaves nothing to be conquered.
   When nothing needs to be conquered, No-boundary is known.
   When no-boundary is known, it allows the country to exist.
   The country, existing from its source, can endure.

3. This is the Tao of having a deep root, a strong stem, a long
   life and an enduring vision.

Chapter 60

1. Governing a large country is like cooking a small fish.
2. If Tao is utilized to manage the society, its ghost will not become spirit.
   Not that ghost is not spiritual, but that the spirit harms no people;
   Not only does the spirit harms not the people, but that the sage is harmless.

3. As those two cause no harm, they are united in Action.

Chapter 61

1. A great nation flows downwardly; it is the mother of the world,
   and the integration of the world.

2. The mother is always tranquil and overcomes the male by her tranquility;
   so she benefits the world.

3. A great nation relies on a low position to take over a small nation.
   A small nation, being in a low position, is taken over by a great nation.

4. So being lower allows taking over or being taken over.
5. Being a great nation only desires to unify the people.
   Being a small nation only seeks people's business.

6. They both get what they want, but the greater is being lower.

Chapter 62

1. Tao is the conductor of all things.
   The treasure of the good.
   The protector of the bad.

2. Beautiful words can advertise well.
   Noble conduct brings praise to people.

3. As for those who conduct the bad, why reject them for it?
4. Therefore, after the crowning of the emperor
   comes the appointing of three administrations.
   Being presented with jade in front of the team of four horses
   is not better than sitting and entering thus.

5. The reason why this is valued of old is,
   It allows having without asking, and it allows forgiveness of wrong.
   Thus, it is most valuable to the world.

Chapter 63

1. Do non-doing.
   Engage in non-affairs. Savor non-flavor.

2. Large or small, many or few, reward or punishment,
   are all being done through Action.

3. Seek what is difficult with ease.
   Effect what is great while it is small.

4. The most difficult things in the world are done while they are easy.
   The greatest things in the world are done while they are small.

5. The sage never plans to do a great thing.
   Thus, he accomplishes what is great.

6. Facile promises necessarily result in little trust.
   What is easy necessarily entails difficulty.

7. Thus the sage, through extreme trials, encounters no difficulty.

Chapter 64

1. It is easy to sustain what is at rest.
   It is easy to plan for that of which there is not even a sign.
   What is fragile is easily broken.
   What is minute is easily dispersed.

2. Act upon it before it exists.
   Regulate it before it becomes chaos.

3. A massive tree grows from a little sprout.
   A nine-story-building rises from a clod of earth.
   A thousand-fathoms begin with a single step.

4. Those who impose action upon it will fail.
   Those who cling to it lose it.

5. So the sage, through non-action, does not fail.
   Not clinging, he does not lose.

6. The common people's engagement in affairs fail prior to success.
7. So the saying goes, "Give as much careful attention to the end as to the beginning;
   then the affairs will not fail."

8. It is on that account that the sage desires not to desire
   and does not value goods that are hard to get.
   He learns not to learn and restores the common people's losses.
   He is able to support the nature of all things and,
   not by daring, to impose action.

Chapter 65

1. Those who practiced Tao in olden times did not enlighten people,
   Rather they made them simple.

2. What makes it the hardest to govern the people is what they already know.
   It becomes most difficult to govern people because of their knowledge.

3. So, using knowledge to govern the country,
   knowledge itself becomes the thief of the country.
   Not using knowledge to govern the country,
   knowledge itself is the Action of the country.

4. Always realize that these two are the model for ruling.
   Always be aware that this model is the mystic Action.

5. Mystic Action is deep and far-reaching.
   It is the opposite of matter.
   Only thus does it approach the Great Harmony.

Chapter 66

1. The reason why rivers and seas have the capacity for kingship over all the valleys
   is that they excel in lowliness.
   That is why they have the capacity for kingship over all valleys.

2. Thus, since the sage wants to elevate the people, his speech is down to earth.
   Since the sage wants to advance the people, he positions himself at the back,

3. So that when he is at the front, people do not harm him.
   When he stands above, people do not feel pressure.
   The whole world supports him untiringly.

4. Since he does not rely on competition,
   the world has nothing with which to compete.

Chapter 67

1. A small country has few people.
2. Weapons are far more numerous than the people, but they are not used.
   Let people be serious about death and enjoy a long journey.
   Though there are carriages and boats, they are not useful for travel.
   Let people return to:
   Use the technique of knotting the rope,
   Enjoying the food,
   Appreciating the cloth,
   Delighting in customs,
   Settling into their living conditions.

3. The neighbouring countries are in sight.
   The sounds of dogs and chickens are heard.
   People grow old and die without interference from each other.

Chapter 68

1. Trustworthy words are not beautiful.
   Beautiful words are not trustworthy.
   The knower does not know everything.
   The know-it-all knows nothing.
   Kindness is not over-indulgent.
   Over-indulgence is not kind.

2. The sage does not collect.
   As soon as he exists for others, he has more.
   As soon as he gives to others, he has more.

3. So the Tao of heaven benefits and does not harm.
   The Tao of human-kind exists and does not compete.

Chapter 69

1. Everyone in the world says I am great, great without parallel.
   Being without parallel is what enables greatness.
   If there is a long standing parallel, it becomes small.

2. I always have three treasures:
   First is compassion.
   Second is frugality.
   Third is to not dare act in front of the world.

3. So compassion enables courage.
   Frugality enables abundance.
   Not daring to act in front of the world enables the mechanism to endure.

4. Today there is courage without compassion.
   There is abundance without frugality.
   There is appearance alone without substance.
   This means no-life.

5. Through compassion: fight and win; defend and be secure.
6. When the heaven establishes itself, it always relies upon compassion.

Chapter 70

1. Being a good warrior does not entail power.
   A good fighter is not angry.
   One who is good at overcoming the enemy does not contact him.
   One who is good at leading people acts humbly.

2. This is called the Action of non-competition.
   This is called leading people.
   This is called the Ultimate as old as heaven.

Chapter 71

1. There is a saying on using military force, it says:
   I dare not be the host, but rather a guest.
   I dare not advance an inch, but rather retreat a foot.

2. This is called performing without performing,
   rolling up one's sleeves without showing the arms.
   By not holding on to an enemy, there is no enemy.

3. There is no disaster greater than having no enemy.
   Having no enemy almost destroys my treasure.

4. When opposing armies clash, those who cry win!

Chapter 72

1. My words are easy to understand and easy to apply.
   Yet no one in the world can understand them and no one could apply them.

2. Words have their origin, and events have their leader.
3. Only because of prevailing ignorance that I am not understood.
   The few who understand me, the more precious I am.

4. So the sage wears shabby cloth, but holds a treasure within.

Chapter 73

1. Knowing that you don't know (everything) is superior.
   Not knowing that you don't know (everything) is a sickness.

2. So the sage's being without sickness is that he knows sickness as sickness;
   Thus, he is without sickness.

Chapter 74

1. People are fearless before the power.
   If fear arises, it will be a great fear.

2. Not constraining the living environment. They do not get bored by life.
   Because we do not get bored, there is no boredom.

3. Therefore the sage is self-aware but not introspective.
   He has self-respect but does not price himself.

4. He rejects one and takes the other.

Chapter 75

1. Courage combined with daring promotes killing.
   Courage not combined with daring promotes life.

2. These two can be either beneficial or harmful.
3. Who knows the reason for what heaven hates?
4. The Tao of heaven is
   Good at winning without fighting,
   Good at responding without speaking,
   Appearing without being asked,
   Good at strategizing while fighting.

5. The net of heaven is broad and loose,
   Yet nothing slips through.

Chapter 76

1. Whenever people are unafraid of death, how can killing be used as a threat?
   Whenever people are afraid of death and are acting contrary,
   I will catch and kill them; who else can act so?
   When people are absolutely afraid of death but perform killing,
   they are the best qualified to be executioners.

2. This is like doing carving for a master craftsman.
   Doing the carving for a master craftsman, how could one's hand not get cut?

Chapter 77

1. The reason people are starving is because the government taxes too much.
   This is the reason for starvation.
   The reason people are hard to govern is because their leaders are actively engaged.
   This is why they are hard to govern.
   The reason people are not serious about death is because they
   seek the burdens of life. This is why they are not serious about death.

2. Only those who are not slaves to life are wise to the value of life.

Chapter 78

1. When people are born, they are soft and gentle.
   When they die, they are stiff and callous.

2. When myriad things, grasses and trees, are born, they are soft and tender.
   When they die, they are withered.

3. So stiffness and callousness are the company of death.
   Softness and suppleness are the company of life.

4. The powerful army will not win.
   A stiff tree will break.

5. So stiffness and power stay below.
   Softness and suppleness stay above.

Chapter 79

1. The Tao of heaven is like drawing a bow.
   The high bends down, the low rises up.
   The surplus decreases.
   Insufficiency is supplied.

2. So the Tao of heaven reduces what is surplus and enhances what is insufficient.
   The human Tao reduces what is insufficient and caters to the surplus.

3. Who can use the surplus to benefit the heaven?
   Only those who possess Tao.

4. So the sage
   Exists without ownership,
   Accomplishes without holding on.
   It is thus, without desire, that the wise see.

Chapter 80

1. Nothing in the world is softer and more supple than water.
   When confronting strength and hardness nothing can overcome it.

2. Using nothingness simplifies.
   Using water overcomes hardness.
   Using weakness overcomes strength.
   There is no one in the world who does not know it, but no one can apply it.

3. So it is a saying of sages that:
   Whoever can bear the disgrace of the country is the ruler of the country.
   Whoever can bear the misfortune of the world is the ruler of the world.

4. Truthful speech seems paradoxical.

Chapter 81

1. Reconciling a great hatred necessarily entails unsolved hatred. How can this be kind?

2. So the sage honors the left-hand tally but does not blame people.
3. Before the kind Action, holds onto the tally.
   Before the kindness Action, holds onto the openness.

4. The Tao of heaven is impersonal. It enhances those who are kind.

Tao Calligraphy Soul Light (Ling Guang)
This image has healing energy embedded in it.

The *Source Ling Guang (Soul Light) Calligraphy* art carries matter (*Jing*), energy (*Qi*), and soul (*Shen*) of *The Source*, which can heal and transform the matter (*Jing*), energy (*Qi*), and soul (*Shen*) of the spiritual, mental, emotional, and physical bodies. – *Dr. Master Zhi Gang Sha, Master Soul Healer*

Courtesy of Bill Gladstone's book *Miracle Soul Healer Documenting a Legend*, 2022
and Dr Master Zhi Gang Sha's book *Soul Healing Miracles*, 2013
Please read *Tao Calligraphy and Tao Song*, page 57
Enlightenment is possible through Tao calligraphy and Tao songs by removing blockages. – Ricardo B Serrano

The ultimate goal is to get to the Kong (Kung) - an enlightenment state - which is the moment when you enter total Emptiness or Nothingness and bliss even if it just for a split moment. It is called Sunya in Sanskrit and the Void in modern terms, however, most people do not realize that this "nothing-ness" is really referring to the spiritual nature of the universe. *What you write and chant is what you become.* - Master Sha

Epilogue

According to ancient Chinese myth, earth's generative natural process takes the form of dragon. Dragon animates all things in an unending cycle of life and death and rebirth, and revered as the force of life itself. Ancient Chinese spirituality was a matter of belonging to dragon's realm which traces its source back to the origins of Taoist philosophy and mystic philosophers such as Chuang Tzu and Lao Tzu.
After a legendary encounter of Confucius, Chinese philosopher, with Lao Tzu, he exclaimed:
"A dragon mounting wind and cloud to soar through the heavens -- such things are beyond me. And today, meeting Lao Tzu, it was like facing a dragon."

I consider ancient Taoist sages such as Lao Tzu and Chuang Tzu, and all ascended masters from different traditions as dragons because their consciousness have merged with the Source of All There Is -- the Tao or Spirit, from whence they came. Even though the models used by masters from varied traditions to attain Oneness are different, the goal of self-realization and ascension is common and the same among them. The models under discussion in this book and epilogue is the 5,000 year old Taoist model of meditation and cultivation of Te (virtue energy) expounded by Taoist Masters Mantak Chia and Tao Huang through Supreme Taoist Master Lao Jung Tzu's Tao Te Ching.

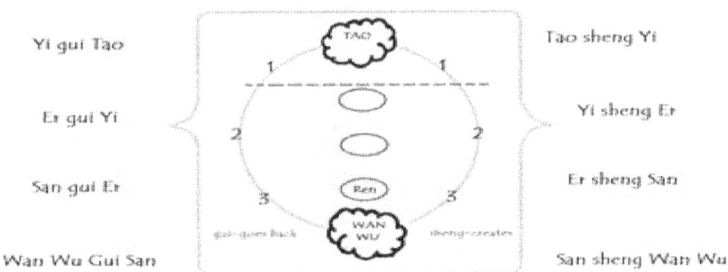

Tao Normal Creation and Reverse Creation
Grand Unification Theory - Tao Science
for Healing, Rejuvenation, Longevity and Immortality

The Neidan (inner alchemy) Meditation taught by Master Mantak Chia and Master Tao Huang's cultivation of Te (virtue energy) from their book *Door to All Wonders, Application of Tao Te Ching*, and Michael Winn's Primordial Qigong with Kan and Li Qigong are excellent models to gather, circulate and store Chi and open your heart to unconditional love and other virtues. From the earliest days of the Taoist tradition the practice of nourishing the vitality of the body has been a central concern, a concern that was elaborately developed in the Taoist tradition of inner alchemy (neidan) later known as the golden elixir (jindan). The foundations of internal alchemy practices can be found in the cosmogony set forth in chapter 42 of the Tao Te Ching:
"Tao gives rise to One; One gives rise to Two; Two gives rise to Three; Three gives rise to all things." This cosmogony accounts for the gradual decay and dissipation of energy within the cosmos. The aim of the alchemist is to reverse this dissipation by reverting or countering (ni) the cosmogonic process, a process further elaborated in terms of the cyclical mutation of yin into yang and yang into yin, as symbolized in the sixty-four hexagrams of the I Ching (Book of Changes) which in turn can be demonstrated to have a direct relation to the human genetic code. Briefly, the aim is to arrive, through a series of purifications, at the decoction of undifferentiated yang- and yin-energy (the "Two" of the cosmogonic sequence), and to fuse these two primal energies into the undifferentiated Oneness of the original Tao.

According to Tao Master Zhi Gang Sha's book "Soul Mind Body Medicine: The Grand Unification Theory for Healing, Rejuvenation, Longevity and Immortality (2014), See photo, page 47, the Tao Normal Creation and Reverse Creation: *Tao Normal Creation* states, "*Tao sheng yi, yi sheng er, er sheng san, san sheng wan wu,*" which means Tao creates One. One creates Two. Two creates Three. Three creates countless things. The *Tao Reverse Creation* states, "*Wan Wu Gui San, San Gui Er, Er Gui Yi, Yi Gui Tao,*" which means "Gui" means return or go back. In every moment, Wan Wu goes back to Three. Three goes back to Two. Two goes back to One, the Hun Dun.

Tao Normal Creation and Tao Reverse Creation is the highest wisdom and highest practice. In Tao teaching, everyone and everything is made of jing qi shen. "Jing" means matter. "Qi" means energy. "Shen" includes soul, heart, and mind. Mind means consciousness. The sacred Tao oneness formula mantra is *Shen (S) + Energy (E) + Matter (M) = 1*, or *Shen Qi Jing He Yi (join as one)*.

The mantra Ren Di Tian Tao Shen Qi Jing He Yi means human being, Mother Earth, Heaven, Tao and Shen Qi Jing join as One. Visualize Golden Ball of Light the size of universe rotating in Lower Abdomen while chanting Ren Di Tian Tao Shen Qi Jing He Yi, read Tao Meditation, pages 51, 66, 71-72

Condense the Original Spirit (Yuan Shen) in the lower abdomen and regulate the breath. – Chang San-Feng

According to Master Tao Huang, "*The teaching focuses essentially on the purification of Jing-Chi-Shen into its final product: the elixir of pure-person. Jing is interpreted as the essence of our biophysical body. Chi manifests as psycho-personal energy between body and spirit. Shen represents the cosmic/wisdom spirit. The elixir is the practice that manifests as the true self.*

The complete Taoist pilgrimage consists of learning the process of planting a seed of pure-person in our two mystic fields: body and soul. This is accomplished through the practice of gathering, circulating and crystallizing the yin-yang chi of the universe in our energy centers: cauldron (thymus/heart), Yellow Court (navel), and crown. Through this practice of calming the desire of the heart, abandoning the minding mind, and tranquilizing the confused spirit, these three conscious realms will be unified into one-spirit within the cosmic void.

In order to merge three into one, we must be in harmony, with two. Just as the book Tao Te Ching has two distinct sections, Tao and Te, our spiritual practice concerns the application of the seed of Tao - spirit self, and the kind action of Te - virtuous deeds. As the seed and love become one, we are our true spirit." To be a true spiritual channel as exemplified by Master Lao Tzu's wisdom through his classic Tao Te Ching, spiritual balance is necessary between gathering, circulating and storing heavenly and earth Chi in our body through meditation, and cultivating (Te) virtuous deeds such as kind action, faith, love and compassion.

According to Master Tao Huang "*Tao is based on meditation; Te is rooted in cultivation. Meditation is for the body/mind whereas cultivation is a treatise on virtue and conscious mind. To meditate is to gather and circulate Chi; to cultivate is to abandon the ego and to purify the consciousness. In Taoist inner alchemy, they are equally important. The practice of distilling the mind can appear daunting when the body is truly hungry. It would be equally unmanageable to purify the body if the mind was not fully prepared to offer the proper environment.*

During meditation and cultivation practice, both Tao and Te tread the same path during the inhalation since Te has not yet been suffused. The Tao suffuses above the sky and inside nothing. Once the Tao of eternal seed is born, the descending order is complete and the action of Te takes place. It is the arrival of the ascending order of returning; exalting and honoring one's own action that rises above physical and mental attachment. Lingering in this action is the Chi: energy of love and breath."

I believe that love, compassion, kindness and faith are the greatest assets in spiritual practice.

According to Master Tao Huang, *"When the nature of selflessness is restored through the meditation of Love, the output of action is in itself kind and trustworthy, beyond what the rational mind has defined. The reliability of truth is to follow the mental configuration of truth and to trust the reality of possible change of truth. The process is kind and the inner quality is trustworthy due to the transformation of Love and the total respect of Inner-Love. When the universal loving energy is gathered within, the biological need and psychological satisfaction are fulfilled, thereby leaving no room within the body and mind for desire and demand created by ego. Self-trust is established and conscious fear is relinquished.*

When the sage (pure-person) uses the universal loving energy, his action is both kind and trustworthy as Lao Tzu has stated. 'He is kind to those who are kind and he is also kind to those who are not kind. It is the kindness of Action itself. He is trustworthy to those who are trustworthy and he is also trustworthy to those who are not trustworthy. It is the trust of Action itself.' "

In closing, I hope that I have conveyed through this book the importance of Lao Tzu's four techniques – *"emptying the mind, vitalizing the stomach, softening the will, and strengthening the character."* "Emptying the mind" requires a complete realization of self before the mind can become tranquil. Only when the mind is empty will the body be filled with love and the spirit be able to present itself. "Vitalizing the stomach" is filling the navel with purified Chi through Taoist internal alchemy (neidan) meditation exercises. "Softening the will" is the process of fully accepting the body/mind by diminishing the ego anticipation: the will of self deception/punishment. And finally, "strengthening the character" through the cultivation of Te (virtue energy). Virtuous deeds such as love, compassion, kindness and faith are the greatest assets in spiritual practice. These four techniques are the key to becoming a dragon (divine medium) and the key to open the door to all wonders. According to *Master Sha's Sacred Tao Wisdom*:

The final Key to open the door to all wonders is through Tao Yan Guang with Tao Ling Guang Calligraphy.

Shen which is the presence of "light in the eyes" is strengthened through contemplative practices such as meditation, Qigong and Tao calligraphy. Master Sha's *Tao (Eye Light) Yan Guang Calligraphy* is a powerful practice that Tao masters use to directly replenish the *Yuan Qi*, *Yuan Jing* and *Yuan Shen* of the eyes to transform soul journey, heal any illnesses and enlighten the physical, mental, emotional and spiritual bodies. *The light of the body is the eye: if thine eye be single, thy whole body shall be full of light.* – Christ; The purpose of Tao wisdom is to build our Soul Lightbody to reach higher dimensions and Tao Source to heal and transform.

The Taoist model discussed in this book is all about experience. I believe that the only way to gauge the truth of any model of enlightenment including Master Lao Tzu's Tao Te Ching is what rings true to you and not what anybody says including me. What rings true to me is what I spiritually experience when I contemplate the passages of the classic and practice Taoist inner alchemy meditation techniques. I concur with Master Tao Huang when he said, *"The only choice to be made is to follow in the footsteps of a sage, going backward, and being One with the Tao. It is not another mandatory rule; it is reverting to the original unified nature where we are meant to be. The life of a sage creates no social ramification since he lives beyond social qualification and cultural limitation. This is why being One with Tao means abandoning the egoistic mind and self-inhibited culture."*

The reason why I have written this book Return to Oneness with the Tao and why I am recommending Master Lao Tzu's Tao Te Ching is the realization after my self-realization and ascension experience that I needed a time-tested proven guidebook and reference from a true sage. After reading Master Tao Huang's English translation of Master Lao Tzu's classic and experiencing a direct connection with Master Lao Tzu's mind and energetic vibration, I knew then that he is a sage. I also realized from my spiritual experiences the truism of his statement "*The Tao of heaven is impersonal. It enhances those who are kind*." When there is Love within, there is enough kindness, compassion, and generosity. Ego is transformed into the stillness of heart, the wisdom of mind, and the tranquility of spirit. Whether you want to be embraced by the light of Love and harmony of Tao - the sweet dew between heaven and earth or think only with your head is entirely your own choice.

"Being at peace, one can see into the subtle.
Engaging with passion, one can see into the manifest.
They both arise from a common source but have different names.
Both are called the mystery within the mystery.
They are the door to all wonders." - Lao Tzu

Ten Da (Greatest) Qualities of Tao Source are carried by Tao Calligraphy and Tao Songs. Read pages 46, 57

Key Terms and Notes

The Tao Te Ching is divided traditionally into two parts: Tao Ching (The Classic Way) and Te Ching (The Classic of Action / Integrity / Virtue).

Tao: Way

> As the generative ontological process through which all things arise and pass away, Tao might be divided into being (the ten thousand things of the empirical world in constant transformation) and nonbeing, the generative source of being and its transformation. Inner voice is the most sacred spiritual vessel. Without this inner voice, God is not alive, The Tao is not present, and the self is not active.

To establish a clear relationship with this sacred vessel, do the following exercises:

1. Listen intently to the sound of silence: a combination of spiritual voice and personal voice.
2. Pay attention to the most immediate direction and clear message: the manifestation of your inner voice.
3. Verbalize it inwardly, whether or not it makes sense to you.
4. Name it with no preconceived notion.
5. Meditate upon it as a part of the visionary journey of your life before it actually takes place.
6. Connect your own name with it. See how it conforms to you, your personality.
7. Make it work for you. It is the divine plan and your decision must be made now.

> When the hands, heart and mind are unified, the inner voice speaks itself. We inhale the power of Tao into our life and return it with the virtue of Te.
>
> *Tao is very close, but everyone looks far away. Life is very simple, but everyone seeks difficulty.* – Lao Tzu, Taoist sage, 200 B.C.
>
> According to Master Sha's book *Soul Mind Body Medicine Grand Unification Theory: Tao is Yuan Shen. Yuan Shen is Tao. Yuan Shen is hidden in your Ming Men area.*
>
> "Melding Shi Shen with Yuan Shen is why soul healing miracles happen." – Ricardo B Serrano
>
> Chant: *Yuan Shen forgives me. Yuan Shen removes soul mind body blockages. Yuan Shen rejuvenates me. I align with my Yuan Shen. I meld with my Yuan Shen. How blessed I am. Yuan Shen is within me. Yuan Shen is Tao. Tao is the Creator. The Creator is within me. I love my Yuan Shen. I honor my Yuan Shen. Everyone has Yuan Shen. I love you, my Yuan Shen. I honor you, my Yuan Shen. I am happy to ask Yuan Shen to heal me. I am honored to ask Yuan Shen to bless all of my life. I want to meld with my Yuan Shen. Ren Di Tian Tao Shen Qi Jing He Yi.* (Ren Di Tian Tao Shen Qi Jing He Yi means *human being, Mother Earth, Heaven, Tao and Shen Qi Jing join as One.*)

- Te: Action / Integrity / Virtue

  Action / Integrity / Virtue to Tao in the sense of "abiding by the Way," or "enacting the Way." It is Tao's manifestation in the world, especially in a sage master of Tao. When the sage (pure-person) uses the universal loving energy, his action is both kind and trustworthy. Through Love, *kind action* becomes endless, inexhaustible, and unfathomable. Lao Tzu emphasized that *eminent Te is like a valley*, since *valley-spirit is deathless*. *Kind action* is the very nature of Mother's power of creative nourishment: a combination of selfless love and self-sacrifice.

- Mu, etc: Mother

  The philosophy of Tao embodies a cosmology rooted in that most primal and wondrous presence: earth's mysterious generative force. This represents a resurgence of the cosmology of late Paleolithic and early Neolithic cultures, where this force was venerated as the Great Mother. She continuously gives birth to all creation, and like natural process which she represents, she also takes life and generates it in an unending cycle of life, death, and rebirth. In Tao Te Ching, this awesome generative force appears explicitly in Lao Tzu's recurring reference to the female principle in a variety of manifestations: mother, valley spirit, female, feminine, yielding, source, origin, etc. But in the end, it is everywhere in the Tao Te Ching, for it is nothing other than Tao itself.

  Shi Shen is a person's body soul located in the heart. *Shi Shen* is our soul that reincarnates. Sacred wisdom says another soul is created by Tao Source during conception. The soul is named *Yuan Shen*. *Yuan Shen is Tao. Tao is Yuan Shen. The true boss is Yuan Shen*. The moment your *Shi Shen* recognizes *Yuan Shen*, you have reached enlightenment that is called *soul enlightenment*.

  Invoke Yuan Shen and you could receive soul healing miracles.

NOTES:

1 mystery within a mystery is the door to all wonders: This mystery is where the center, the medium, and the equilibrium embrace, balance, and unify from both sides and both ends, while maintaining the middle ground. It is where the emulation, competition and perfection face their extremes and opposites in a peaceful manner, and where beauty and ugliness no longer appear attractive or repulsive, where good and bad are no longer distinctive. The door is an eye opening and a conscious connection with the wonders of the universe, or God's creation. The 'Door' functions as a middle point between the internal world and the external world, between the information within and without ¾ or between those who have been initiated, ordained, or baptized and who have the gifts of God but have not established a cosmic bridge within themselves. In order to open the door, the readiness of the heart and completion of purification must take place first.

Otherwise, the heart-sealed teachings between the teacher and student cannot begin. Ultimately, the door refers to a specific realm of consciousness of God, a line connecting two sides, or a flowing river covering both sides of the riverbed. Shoel is the word in the Bible. Taking another example, Shakespeare's plays are doors, which are carried out either by readers and writers, or between stage players and audience. This is the precise functioning of a door, a cosmic vehicle connecting heart and mind, Xing and Ming, soul and spirit.

5 straw dogs: scarecrows.

heaven and earth: heaven and earth might be conceived as "creative force and created objects."

10 qi: the universal breath, vital energy, or life-force.

gate of heaven: gateway through which the ten thousand things come into being and return to nothing.

11 Thirty spokes join at one hub: 30 spokes refer to the 5 facial organs, 5 internal organs, 10 fingers and 10 toes. The one hub is the one spinal column of vertebrae, particularly the tailbone which connects to the heart center.

41 Tao moves by returning: returning is the cornerstone of being a Taoist. Only through the inner alchemy practice can we find the way to becoming one with the Tao.

50 three and ten: represents a genetically coded and cosmically numbered journey of life within the completion of ten and trial function of birth, life and death. Ten in Chinese culture represents the completion of numerical functioning coming after nine, which is the biggest and highest cardinal number. Ten and three represent the numerical order of universal manifestation.

54 thus: awareness of self and universe by being one with the creative force.

72 holds a treasure within: the inner child, the pure self, the God-like self.

> *"Tao is based on meditation; Te is rooted in cultivation.*
> *Meditation is for the body/mind whereas cultivation is a treatise*
> *on virtue and conscious mind. To meditate is to gather and circulate Chi;*
> *to cultivate is to abandon the ego and to purify the consciousness."*
> *—Door to All Wonders*

According to my Sri Vidya Guru, Sri Amritananda Natha, Sri Devi: Hindus call her Gayatri, Christians call her the Virgin Mary, Buddhists call her the Compassion, Sufis call her the Movement; other ancient religions simply call her Mother Earth. She is our source, our sustenance and our end. She is Kundalini, the power moving us toward the unity of all life.

She combines in Herself the tenderness of all mothers and the passion of all lovers, wisdom and insanity, childishness and experience, cruelty and faithfulness.

She is maya; dissolution of maya leads to mahasamadhi from which there is no return. This is the reason why it is insisted that you treat Devi as your mother; then the thought of enjoying Her does not arise that easily in the head, preserving your life. But think! what better way to die than in the hands of mother, to become Shiva, a death like corpse? If you are Her child, She feeds you with milk from Her ever full breasts; and the milk of life is sweet indeed. But in the total recognition there is no second – one does indeed become Shiva and Shakti in union; then there is no manifest world, except the continuous unending bliss. And one who has once tasted the sweetness of it, does not want to come back, except as a sacrifice of freedom brought about willfully! Om Aeem Hreem Shreem Namaha! See page 112, Oneness with Shiva

Commentary on I Ching (Book of Changes)

The following commentary is a simplified presentation of basic information and concepts relating to the I Ching and the genetic code (DNA) derived from the book *Door to All Wonders*. This will benefit readers who are not conversant in these areas and their interrelatedness. This will smooth the way to appreciate the practical significance of textual explanations that often refer to the I Ching. The reason for this presentation is that it has been recognized that the 5000-year-old I Ching 'world formula' correlates 'exactly' to the structure and dynamics known of the modern genetic code (DNA). This understanding translates in practical terms to our understanding of how and why our meditation practices have powerful benefits at the cellular level of inner alchemy for health and spiritual transformation.

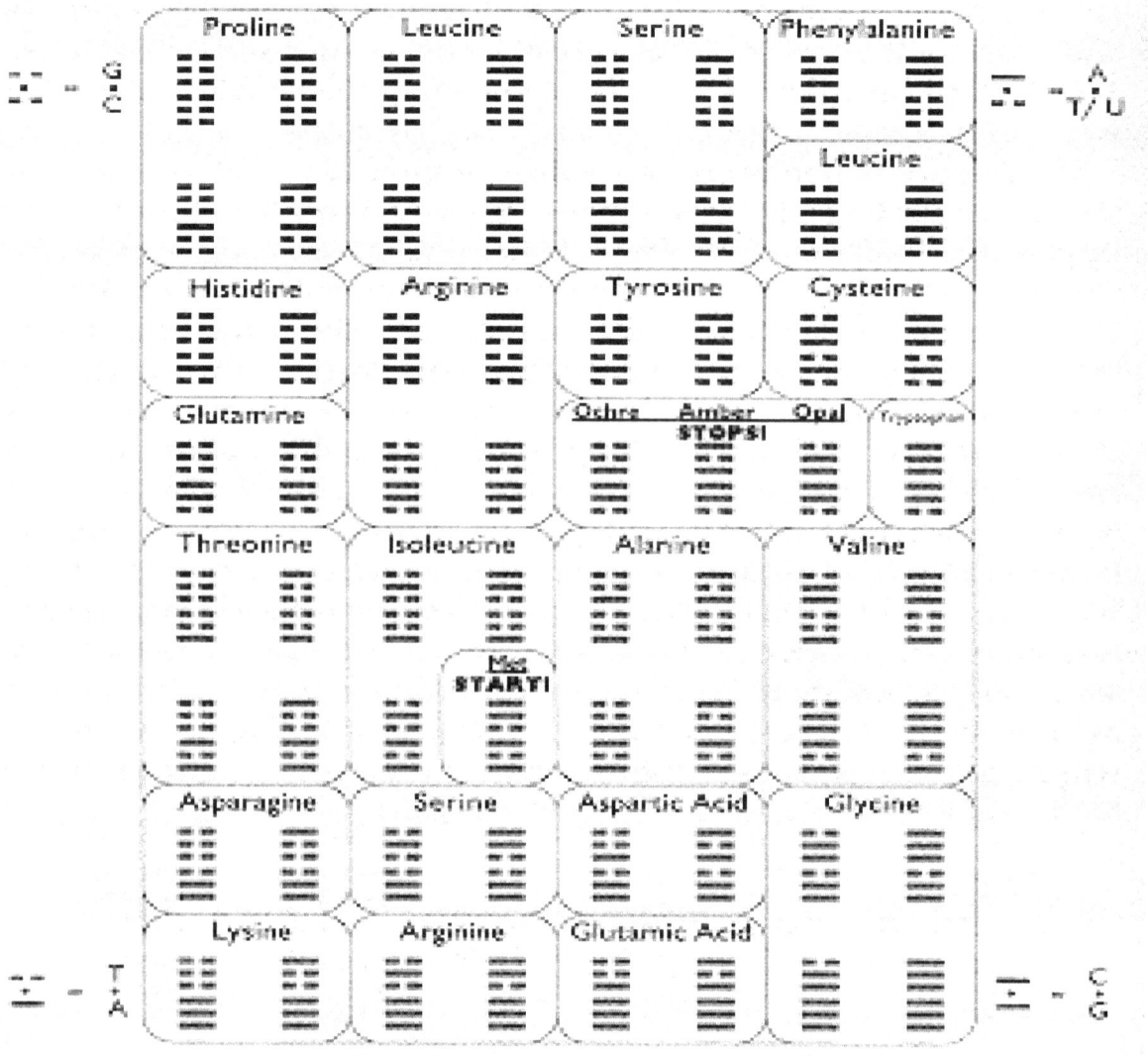

Genetic Code and the I Ching 64 Hexagrams

- *"Due to the tremendous advances in genetic science, it is inspiring to have a sense of how we come to be the way we are. Consequently, it may also support us in our practices to know that we really do have the capability to profoundly influence our health and evolution. By getting the good biosignals humming and riding up and down those spiral stairways in our DNA, activating those good codons in our cells, transforming spirit from matter, and at the same time enhancing the quality and significance of our physical being -- who knows what limits we may transcend.*

- *The key to the structure and dynamics of life in our genes is the same as the I Ching's 64 dynamic states of tension between the polar opposites of yin and yang. It is the same as the wisdom, the cosmology of the world, embodied in the I Ching that was compiled 5,000 years ago by Fu-Hsi. By comparing the charts of Fu-Hsi's hexagrams and the Genetic Code's triplet codons, feel a sense of awe for the beauty and power of truth in the microcosm in each of the trillions of cells in your body. As well, sense the polar connection with the complementary primordial Chi of the universe, the macrocosm.*

- *Be like Neils Bohr, one of the godfathers of the modern science of the subatomic world -- quantum physics. The result of his work and others has confirmed the dual polarity nature of the wave/particle reality in the subatomic realm of existence. After he had already elaborated his interpretation of quantum theory -- when he visited China in 1937, he was deeply impressed by the ancient Chinese notion of the complementary of polar opposites, which paralleled his thinking. So much so, that when he was knighted in his native Denmark in 1947 in acknowledgement of his outstanding achievements -- he chose the Tai Chi symbol and the inscription 'Opposites are complementary" for the motif of his coat-of-arms. Create your coat-of-arms in your body's consciousness in the core of your cells and manifest your body wisdom. The purpose of our Taoist practices is to enable us to be healthy, happy, conscious, evolving human beings and thereby be able to achieve life beyond life."*

The source for longevity is within the body, not as a physical womb but a spiritual one. Taoists call this spiritual womb "cauldron." The right method to "cook the cauldron" is not to search outwardly for love from others, but to search within the naked and abandoned self. It is the method of going back to the state in which we are all orphans, in the very depth of our body/minds." - Door to All Wonders

Application of the Internal Alchemy (Neidan) of the Tao

I would like to start with an excerpt of Master Tao Huang's commentary from his book *"Door to All Wonders"*:

"I was very happy, and felt very fortunate that I was able to have Lao Tzu as my Spiritual Master. This became the foundation for me to become a true Taoist. I could now practice Taoism not simply from personal beliefs, but from personal connection to and embracement with a real Master. "The heart-sealed teaching is the essential method in neidan practice. Just like a married couple, each is barren, having only half of the complete heart. When the teacher's heart and student's heart become one, or two souls become one pure spirit, the teachings are given and taken in their own way. This has been characterized by the eighth hexagram in I Ching, where two heads are cut off- only the two half-hearts merge into oneness. Essentially it is about two nines, one for our spirit/soul, and the other the cosmic/God consciousness. The oneness is the combination of white of seed/God consciousness and yellow court/sprout of spirit self. [More discussion on I Ching hexagrams is presented in another section herein.]

"Also, when the two hearts reach oneness, you cannot tell which is which. This is the most difficult situation for me to explain: which part of the exercises are inherently Lao Tzu's and which parts are my own understanding or reflection upon his teachings-or revelation.

The Taoists' emphasis has been on creating an open energy space for the cultivation of a natural, spontaneous energy flow as the intuitive awakening and manifestation of that which is intrinsic in the wisdom of the body. Hence, we may observe that in Confucianism, as well as in mainstream modern education, there is a form of domestication of self-reliance, and of multiple originalities of the expression of self. The cultivation of truthful intention, and of inner emotions such as compassion, love, caring, generosity, and service are ignored and repressed. This results in stunting the personal growth and generating an all-pervasive neurosis and stress, as the body protests and seeks to be acknowledged and honored in its true being.

In the Taoist vision of the learning process, the body memory-through which the universe and nature express themselves, and through which we are connected with our biological and spiritual ancestors-is the seat of intuitive awareness and of the mind as consciousness. In this view, the mind consciously mirrors the body. We carry within our body the entire process of the evolution of humankind and its interconnection with the universe and with nature. In its natural state, our body is in resonance with the universe and nature through the very crystalline structure of its bones, its vaults, the feet, the pelvis, the chest, the palate and the cranium, as well as through its glands and organs."
This is an important first step for one to practice in the journey of self-mastery and for attaining spiritual independence and the ultimate goal of spiritual immortality.

(Tao Te Ching, chapter 70, translation by Stephen Mitchell)

My teachings are easy to understand and easy to put into practice. Yet your intellect will never grasp them, and if you try to practice them, you'll fail.
My teachings are older than the world. How can you grasp their meaning? If you want to know me, look inside your heart. - Lao Tzu
      Opening your heart to the unconditional love of the universe (Tao Source) is the way. – Lao Tzu
As a result of my experiences during Tao soul communication with Master Lao Tzu, I concur with Stephen Mitchell's above translation. *"If you want to know the Tao or connect with me, look inside your heart."* – Lao Tzu
By opening your soul communication channels, you can self-heal, attain peace and soul enlightenment, and altogether communicate with the Tao Source, spiritual guides and souls of loved ones to receive guidance and assistance for your health, well-being and everyday life challenges.
The regular application of Soul songs with the five power techniques makes it possible to open your soul communication channels to heal and transform your self and others. – Ricardo B Serrano, Soul Healer, Communicator

Tao Calligraphy by Master *Zhi Gang Sha*

"Each calligraphy I produce contains the frequency of Tao Oneness. I teach this to allow others to learn the principle of Oneness and to share it with others. As the calligrapher, I apply one flow of qi in a single stroke, creating high frequency positive messages.

When we practice Tao Calligraphy through the act of writing, tracing, or meditating within the Tao Calligraphy Healing Field, we align with the very essence of Oneness. This act of sharing and enlightenment through the healing field brings balance into our lives and our world."

Figure 1 Greatest Love

Taoist Immortals

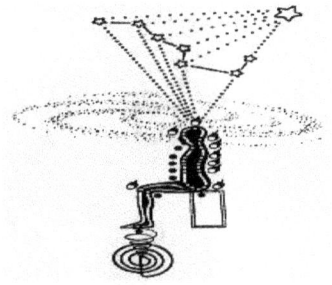

Microcosmic Orbit

Tao Source song (Tao Ge) carries transformative Source love, light, frequency, vibration, energy, and messages. *Tao Calligraphy, Tao Song, Tao Water* are the three most powerful Source technologies for healing and transformation created by *Dr. Master Zhi Gang Sha*. Read *Soul Song Love Peace Harmony*, p. 93
Tao Calligraphy Soul Light (see page 46) healed my chronic foot pain. – Ricardo B Serrano, Soul Healer
To chant Tao is to reach Tao. – Master Sha

Dharanas (Verses) from *Vijnanabhairava* (*Divine Consciousness*)
"All manifestation is not separate from the light of consciousness. The light of consciousness is Never separate from the I-consciousness. The I-consciousness is nothing else than Self and Self is simply pure consciousness." – Verse 137

The essence of Self consists universally in autonomy, bliss, and consciousness. One's absorption in that essence is said to be (real) bath. It is the spiritual bath which consists in a plunge in the essential Self characterized by autonomy, bliss and consciousness that alone can lead to real purification.
– Verse 152

By constant contemplation on the *hamsah* or *so'ham* mantra, one becomes identified with the goddess kundalini and thus through her, one attains the nature of Bhairava. – Verse 155

THE INTERNAL ALCHEMY OF THE TAO
Explanation of the Inner Alchemy Chart

The following neidan (inner alchemy) meditation practice which will gather, circulate and store your (Chi) energy is taught by Taoist Master Mantak Chia derived from his book *Door to All Wonders*:

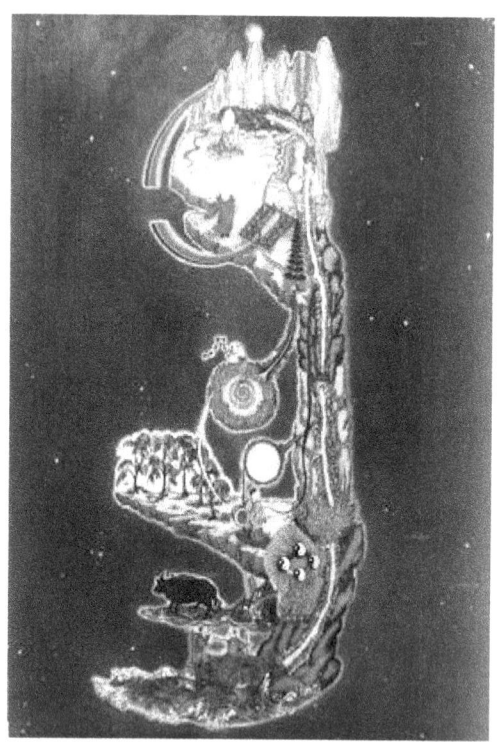

This chart was never copied for over a couple of hundred years. There was only the original. It was never passed down to the rest of the world because it is so profound and mysterious that an ordinary person would have no way to understand it. It was rediscovered in the library at High Pine Tree Mountain in China suspended from the wall. It was carefully drawn and the printing was clear, so it was eventually reprinted at that time. When I first discovered this, I decided to reprint it with a complete explanation using the Healing Tao practices. By practicing the Healing Tao formulas you can start to comprehend the detailed illustrations of this mural connecting with our body and the universe. It is with this understanding that I give you this explanation of Internal Alchemy so beautifully illustrated in this ancient Taoist rendering.

The Tao adept saw human body as a microcosm of the natural world. Its anatomy was a landscape with mountain, river, streams, lake, pool, forest, fire, stars a natural harmoniously landscape. It shows a torso and head with few easily identifiable structures -

The numbered areas 1 to 5 are a series of nine sacred mountain peaks. These mountain peaks are like the funnels, which are able to draw down universal energy. This energy is then concentrated in the caves of the mountains. Taoist adepts go to mountain caves for initiation. In the human head there are nine different centers (peaks or points), which are able to extend to the heaven to make the connection to the cosmos. The cavity in the brain, the body and energy centers are like those caves in a mountain which you can concentrate, store and transform energy.

1. IMMORTAL REALM is located in the center just in front of the crown. It is this point where our energy is able to ascending to heaven making the connection with the heavens drawing down even more powerful universal energies.

2. TOP OF THE GIANT PEAK is located in the back of the head. When we tilt the head and push the Chi back it reaches its highest point. This peak is connected to the North Star and the thymus gland. It is where we receive the descending universal energy.

3. MUD PILL is located in the center of the crown (Bai Hui or the hundredth meeting point) and when it is open it feels like soft mud. The crown point is connected to the Big Dipper and the hypothalamus gland. It is at this center that you can project your energy (soul or spirit) up or receive the energy down giving way to a two way street.

4. HOUSE OF RISING SUN is the third eye. At the middle of the forehead likely above, this center is able to receive the sun and moon energy, and is used to launch the soul and spirit bodies into space travel.

5. NINE PEAKS MOUNTAIN is more directly connected to the mid eyebrow and has a close connection to the pituitary gland. This center is used to received the cosmic force and used for launching the soul and spirit bodies the earthly plan or human plan traveling.

6. OBSCURE SPIRIT ALTER is between the Mud Pill and in front of the Giant Peak where the spirit and soul bodies are leaving and entering into horizontal flight.

7. CAVE OF THE SPIRIT PEAK is the jade pillow between the 1st cervical and the base of the skull which is know as the God mouth where we can receive universal knowledge.

8. TRUE JADE UPPER GATE is a water gate near to throat connecting to the brain.

9. SOURCE OF RISING LAW is behind the soft palate which is connected to the pituitary gland.

9a. The two circles representing the sun and the moon within us are the left and right eyes. By learning how to roll the eyes in a circle motion, we can blend these different energies together enabling us to direct the energies with our eyes. When we roll the eyes up looking to the crown, these energies along with the sexual energy will rise up to the crown. When we roll the eyes down looking to the lower Tan Tien, we bring the premixed energies down to our energy centers (reservoirs) storing them there.

9b. The figure of the old white headed man with eyebrows reaching down to the ground is Lao Tzu (one of the founders of the Taoism). He is a seated figure with long eyebrows which is connected to the earthly energy.

9c. The blue eyed standing foreign monk holds the heaven in his hands. The standing figure is Bodhidharma, the founder of the Zen Buddhism in China, which is holding up his hands to reach the heavens being more connected to the heavenly energy. These two energies or natures are mixed together to form a new Taoist concept, the practice of the Modern Taoism or the Healing Tao system. It is the blending and the harmonizing of our heavenly destiny and our earthly nature.

10. The DRAWBRIDGE is the tongue and the POND OF WATER is the mouth which holds the saliva. In the Taoist practice, when you touch the palate with the tongue (the Source of Rising Law known as the heavenly pool), we connect the circuit forming the link between the governor channel (yang) rising from the perineum up the spine to the head then down to the palate and the conception channel (yin) descending from the root of the lower jaw to the perineum. Once the tongue touches the palate, the Chi is activated. The sexual energy is pumped up to the brain, activating the hypothalamus, pituitary and thymus glands secreting more hormones. The sexual energy, especially the orgasm energy, will help draw in the heaven energy from above and the earth force from below. When you mix these two forces with the sexual energy the hormone secretion is stimulated. This creates an abundance of Chi and fluid. This fluid which flows like a waterfall down through the palate across the upper palate to the back down to the mouth and the throat (Twelve storied pagoda) from where we are able to swallow it down to fill the other two Tan Tiens. This water is also know as the nectar, water of life or the golden elixir.

11. **GOVERNING MERIDIAN** is located from the perineum up the spine to the head then down to the palate.

12. **CONCEPTION OR RELEASING MERIDIAN** is located from the root of the lower jaw to the perineum.

13. **TWELVE STORIED PAGODA** or twelve story tower is the throat center, CV-22. When the sexual energy is pumped up to the crown (reversing the flow) due to the Healing Tao practices of Testicle and Ovarian Breathing, Power Lock, and the Big Draw through the spine to fill the Lower Tan Tien (kidney and sexual centers) (lower reservoir), the Middle Tan Tien (solar plexus and heart center) (middle reservoir), and Upper Tan Tien (brain, and crystal room) (upper reservoir). During its passage through the spine into the brain center the sexual energy is transformed. After the upper reservoir is filled, then the energy flows down the palate through the tongue down the throat into the heart nourishing it.

14. **I TILL MY OWN FIELD** (Tan Tien or Elixir Field). Inside my field is a magical sprout (the immortal fetus or the unborn spirit) that lives 10,000 years. The color of its flowers (opening of the consciousness and the wisdom) resembles gold and they do not wilt. Its seeds are like Jade pebbles. Its fruits are round. To cultivate it, I depend on the earth of the middle palace (the solar plexus). To irrigate it (the sexual energy reverse the flow up to the crown) I depend on the fountain of the upper valley. After much toil, I achieve the Great Tao and stroll freely through the earth becoming an Immortal of Peng Lai Island.

15. **COWHERDER BRIDGE STARS** symbolizes the yang elements of the heart, fire and compassion fire. He looks like a child which we call yang heart. In Taoist Text and the Christian Bible, they refer it as becoming like a child again which is the symbol of spiritual wisdom, innocence and simplicity. Extending out of the cow herder's crown, you find the Big Dipper, which symbolizes the connection of the heart to the heaven seeking harmony with the cosmos. The Taoist regard the Big Dipper as the cosmic timepiece. During the course of the year, the Big Dipper makes a 360 degree rotation pointing to all the stars collecting all the universal power in the Big Dipper's cup.

The law of the heaven is called destiny and the law of the earth is called nature. The harmony between the destiny and the nature is the Tao, the great way. Those who follow the Tao fulfill their spiritual destiny and enjoy the fruit of the earthly nature. The Taoist way of life is to tap into the energies of the heaven and earth while blending and harmonizing them with the human energy in order to cultivate and conserve the vital force in our bodies. Heaven Forces manifest into the celestial energy and its power appears to us as thoughts, consciousness, fate and destiny. Healing Tao is the practice of connecting the heaven (destiny) and the earth (nature) together. Some system or religion separate the heaven and earth into two realm forcing us to choose one.

16. WITHIN THE 50 REALMS IS CONCEALED THE MYSTERIOUS GATEWAY is opposite the heart which has a close relation and connection to the heart that generates the Big Aura protecting the heart and the crown.

17a. LUNG SPIRIT HWA HAO FROM THE EMPTY IS COMPLETED is the power and ability of the lung to totally empty so it can received more. Each inhale and exhale of our body is the breath of the universe expanding and contracting.

17b. HEART SPIRIT TAN YUAN ALSO CALLED GUARDING SPIRIT is located in the liver area.

17c. GALL BLADDER SPIRIT LUNG AU ALSO CALLED MAJESTIC AND BRIGHT is located in the middle of the liver.

17d. LIVER SPIRIT LUNG YIEN ALSO CALLED CONTAINING WISDOM represents the liver, the largest organ of the body as a forest. In Taoism we regard the liver as the controller of the Chi flow. Too much Chi in one place can cause stagnation or congestion, and too little causes weakness and depletion. Both conditions are results of a liver imbalance. The weaver maid (kidneys) also receives the water from the sexual energy, but also makes water which helps the wood (liver) to grow while the liver provides fuel for the heart fire. Each organ is interdependent to each other.

17e. SPLEEN SPIRIT CH'ANG TSAI ALSO CALLED SOUL PAVILION is located in the spleen area.

17f. KIDNEY SPIRIT HSUAN MING ALSO CALLED NOURISHING THE SEEDS. The kidneys store the constitution of inherited energy from our parents.

18. MIDDLE TAN TIEN (heart center) is surrounded by the pericardium's ring of fire.

19. WEAVING MAIDEN CIRCULATES AND TURNS is yin (kidneys and water element) and the cow herder standing above her is yang. The weaving maid has the ability to store energy, and to go inward to maintain quietness. She weaves silk like garments out of moonlight (Moon Light and the Milky Way energies accumulated and stored in the lower Tan Tien) by using the mind with the gently, soft, long and deep breaths like spinning or pulling silk drawing in the cosmic force and weaving into an internal Chi Web or Network. The Chinese legend says that the cow herder and the weaving maid were lovers once, but they neglect their duties and were change into stars and put at the opposite ends of the sky. One night a year, celebrated as the lover's day about September 15, the birds make a bridge (the milky way) across the sky to join them together. Likewise our heart (spirit, fire, compassion fire, love, and destiny) and the kidneys (earth nature, water, sexual energy, and physical body) are separate since the day we were born and never met again. By reuniting again the heart essence (love and compassion fire) and the kidney essence (sexual energy) we can form the immortal fetus giving birth to it and growing it.

20. KIDNEY CAVE (GV-4, Ming Men, Door of Life) is known as the door of fire which is the gate where the sexual energy will pass and help to transform us.

21. CORRECT TAN TIEN (Real Tan Tien) is located in front and below the kidneys just behind the navel closer to the spine.

21a. YIN AND YANG TAN TIEN are the four yin yang symbols represent the Tan Tien area (field of the elixir) located slightly below the navel approximately 3 inches near the sexual center. This area is the first alchemical cauldron. Tai Chi (yin and yang) represents the moving force. By using the mind, eyes and abdominal breathing to move the Chi and accumulate the sexual energy you will start to cook and be transformed it into Chi (steam) flowing through the channels of the entire body to repair and energize the cells.

22. NORTH SEA WATER FLOWS IN REVERSE is located the sacral hiatus (GV-2). When the sexual energy is pumped up to the crown (reversing the flow) due to the Healing Tao practices of Testicle and Ovarian Breathing, Power Lock, and the Big Draw through the spine to fill the Lower Tan Tien (kidney and sexual centers) (lower reservoir), the Middle Tan Tien (solar plexus and heart center) (middle reservoir), and Upper Tan Tien (brain, and crystal room) (upper reservoir). During its passage through the spine into the brain center the sexual energy is transformed. After the upper reservoir is filled, then the energy flows down the palate through the tongue down the throat into the heart nourishing, cooling, and irrigating it.

23. YIN AND YANG MYSTERIOUS WATER WHEEL is located at the perineum. Sexual energy is the most vital life force that humans inherit from their parents. We need this energy (orgasm force) to run our life each day. In the Human way this sexual energy is like water, which tends always to run down and out. Each day we lose this force through sexual desire, greed, or unnecessary worldly materialism. We need to reverse this process causing the sexual energy (water and earth nature) to flow inward and upward. The boy and girl represent the testicles and the ovaries connected to the kidneys and eyes working on the water treadmill step by step pumping the water (sexual energy) upward. This is the beginning of the Healing Love practice with the testicle and the ovarian breathing. By starting to roll the eyes like a ball down the front and up the back, we begin to become aware of the testicles and the ovaries feeling them start rolling together with the eyes. Through this process a sea of sexual energy in the lower Tan Tien will transform into a lighter force flowing upward through the spine to the brain, glands, and organs rejuvenating them.

24. AGAIN AND AGAIN, STEP BY STEP is the yin and yang mystery (the boy and the girl, the testicle and the ovaries, the mind and the eyes) continuously turning the great pumps (the coccyx and the sacrum) to make the water (arousal and orgasm sexual energy) rise to the East (the crown). Even in a lake of 10,000 fathoms (Hui Yin, where all the yin energy of the body meets at the perineum) we should penetrate to the bottom where a sweet spring flows upward to the top of the south mountains (Trusting Meridian starts from the perineum up to the crown, and spreads out from the crown like a spring fountain).

25. THE IRON BULL TILLS THE GROUND AND PLANTS THE GOLDEN COIN is located at the lower Tan Tien around the navel connected to the spleen, ground and the earth connection to the spleen. The spleen center is the seed of the spirit and the life force (Chi). Once we are able to reverse the flow of the sexual energy, we can irrigate the dry land allowing us to till the soil to plant the magical golden sprout producing the golden round fruit

26. THE GOLD COIN. Once the land is ready, the seed of long life and wisdom (the immortal fetus or the gold coin) can be planted. All the land and the plants (our soul, spirit, mind, organs and glands) only need sexual energy to grow. The stone carving child strings them together. In one grain of rice the world mystery is hiding as the human form is the microcosm of the universe) and once we learn to understand and control our mind and ourselves, we will understand the mystery of the universe. In a small pot (either the lower, middle, or upper Tan Tien) we can cook all the mountains and rivers forces (natural forces), stars, moon, and sun forces (universal forces) and the primordial forces (cosmic particles) and combine them within ourselves to transform them into the higher force to form the IMMORTAL FETUS.

Cultivating Qi Energy in the Hara (Lower Dantian)

There are two basic sitting postures for harnessing powerful energy through your vital center. The two sitting postures are either performed crossed leg on the floor or sitting on the edge of a low stool or chair your feet planted on the ground.

Sitting in the crossed leg position is known as the "Lotus posture" and you can sit in either of two variations – half lotus or full lotus. In the sitting posture you will want to place a small cushion of folded towel under your bottom to lift your pelvis. This will slightly tuck the pelvis forward and prevent any strain in your lower back.

Once in the crossed leg position bring your attention to your attention to your head, neck and shoulders. Imagining a taut string attached to the center of the top of your head. Lengthen upward as if a puppeteer is pulling on the string. Neck straight, chin drawn slightly down and inward. Relax your shoulders while inhaling deeply into your hara filling your entire body with fresh, vitalizing Qi.

Your shoulders should remain relaxed. Gently close your eyes halfway and gaze downward about ten feet in front of you. Take a moment to re-check the alignment of your spine. Is your nose aligned with your navel? Are your ears aligned over your shoulders?

One Hand Near, One Hand Far Body Power Technique
- Place the "*Near Hand*" four to seven inches from the area of the body where there is pain, inflammation, or a growth (cyst, tumor). Place the "*Far Hand*" with palm facing the lower abdomen (*Lower Dantien*), fifteen to thirty inches away.
- The *Near Hand* creates a high-density energy field. The *Far Hand* creates a low-density energy field. High density flows to low density. Energy flows from the area that the *Near Hand* faces to the area that the *Far Hand* faces.

For example, if you have a headache in the forehead (*sound Yao or Yi*), place the *Near Hand* four to seven inches in front of the forehead. Place the *Far Hand* fifteen to thirty inches in front of the lower abdomen (*Lower Dantien*), with palm facing the abdomen accompanied with *Sound power Jiu*. *Where you put your hands is where you receive healing and rejuvenation.*

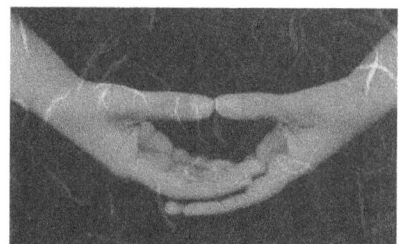

The hands are particularly sensitive to Qi. How they are held during any practice has an influence on how Qi moves in, out and through the human system.

In his classic *Zen Mind, Beginner Mind* Shunryu Suzuki states, "If you put your left hand on top of your right, middle joints of your middle fingers together, and touch your thumbs lightly together (as if you held a piece of paper between them), your hands will make a beautiful oval (photo above) you should keep this universal mudra with great care, as if you were holding something very precious in your hand. Your hands should be held against your body, with your thumbs at about the height of your navel. Hold your arms freely and easily, and slightly away from your body, as if you held an egg under each arm without breaking it."

> "We join spokes together in a wheel, but it is the center hole that makes the wagon move. We shape clay into a pot, but it is the emptiness inside that holds whatever we want. We hammer wood for a house, but it is the inner space that makes it livable. We work with being, but non-being is what we use."
>
>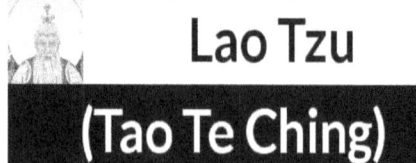
> Lao Tzu
> (Tao Te Ching)

The hands are particularly sensitive to Qi. Hand positions, known as mudra in Sanskrit are regarded as very important aspects of meditation practice. The position of the hands has an influence on the movement of Qi energy.

Remain relaxed and release any muscle tension. Breathe naturally. Your breath will find its pace and you may notice that it naturally slows and deepens. Inhale and exhale through your nose and allow the inbreath to sink deep into your abdomen. Visualize your breath falling into a point just below your navel. This point is the hara (in Japanese), tancheon (in Korean), or dantian (in Chinese).

For thousands of years people in the East have developed methods to gather energy from the dantian. This is the source of primal wisdom and vital energy that resides within each of us. It is considered the *seat of the soul*. Man by his lower dantian is indeed a microcosm of the universe where the soul of the universe can be stored there. Chant the mantra *Jiu Jiu Jiu Jiu Jiu* with the golden ball of light in the lower dantian to boost energy.

Read *One Hand Near, One Hand Far*, page 65; *Tao Immortal Way Breathing*, page 68

Where Your Awareness (Attention) Goes, Energy Follows

Allow your mind to settle on the rhythm of your breathing. Bring your attention fully to your hara (dantian). Each inhalation renews this source of energy while each exhalation draws from it. After ten minutes, you may bring all of your attention to focus on the dantian. It may be helpful to imagine a point of gold light in the dark space of your abdomen.

If your thoughts drift gently direct them back to the rhythm of your breath and unto the golden light at your center. Own that part of your body.

Allow the energy of the hara (dantian) to move up your spine and throughout your body (microcosmic orbit). This energized feeling is peace from being in balance.

It is while cultivating energy from the hara (dantian) that the emptiness of non-doing (wuwei) brings you peace and brings back to your source to your true nature.

Cultivating energy from this center point (dantian) requires consistent practice. Stay humble and move through every moment of each day through your hara.

In the words of scholar Christopher Markert, "When your engage the energy of your dantian, your daily tasks become artful activities in which you joyfully engage your self."

Being focused in your vital center is bliss, while any suffering is simply a communication from your Body and your Mind that you have lost touch with your true nature. In fact, one could even say that you are out of touch with Nature in general and the cosmic life force.

Disclaimer

- The physical and physiological conditions of each practitioner vary. Therefore, the author and publisher will not be liable for any adverse effects arising from the practice of the meditation techniques and exercises given in this book.
- If discomfort(s) or adverse effect(s) are experienced, the practitioner is advised to stop the practice immediately.

NOTE: I would like to thank and acknowledge Sundo Master Hyunmoon Kim, Ron Catabia, and Gracia del Rosario for their articles on Sundo tancheon breathing, Aikido Master Kichi Tohei for his article "Ki in Daily Life," and Cara Michelle Miller for her article "Cultivating Energy in the Hara" she learned while on retreat at the Dai Bosatsu Zen Monastery. *Soul Mind Body Medicine*, *Divine Healing Hands* by Zhi Gang Sha.

According to Tao grandmaster *Dr. Zhi Gang Sha*, "*Zhong* is a space inside the body. The sacred wisdom is that *Zhong space* reflects and connects with every part of the body similar to part of the body (ears or feet) reflects an image of the entire body.
In particular, focusing your mind on *Zhong* (core) could balance the *Five Elements*, which include every system, organ, and cell in the body." Read *chanting mantra Zhong*, page 68

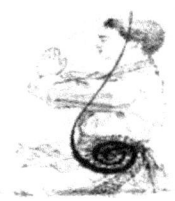

Tao (Immortal Way) Breathing

For best result, practice the above Hara (Dantian) sitting Qigong – another powerful Shaktipat Meditation technique – when under stress, when you're walking, lying down before sleeping; sitting around listening to music, drawing, writing; and especially before and after practicing Wushu (martial arts), the Maitreya (Shiva) Shen Gong elaborated in the Maitreya (Shiva) Shen Gong video and Tao hands with Da Bei Zhou compassion mantra blessing.

Consistent Hara (dantian) Qigong *diaphragmatic* breathing practice – aligned with the middle and upper dantians, in clinical practice, can alleviate high blood pressure, heart diseases, arthritis, breathing and digestive problems, kidney Qi deficiency symptoms, sexual dysfunctions, low vitality or energy (fatigue), insomnia, migraines, various cancers, addictions, and most psychological symptoms caused by too much stress. It is best combined with Qigong, acupuncture, acupressure, Tao healing hands blessing, herbs and psychospiritual counselling for speedy results.
Lastly, it is best to learn this particular Hara (Dantian) sitting or standing Qigong – Tao Breathing – Buteyko breathing - one-on-one from a Qigong expert like me especially if you suffer from chronic diseases, and prevent unnecessary negative side effects caused by the incorrect use of this Hara (Dantian) Qigong with *Zhong* that includes *Kun Gong*, *Ming Men* acupoint, *Wei Lu* and *Hui Yin* acupoint. Read *Buteyko Breathing Method*, page 85
Chant silently or aloud: Zhong Zhong Zhong Zhong Zhong Zhong Zhong Zhong Zhong Zhong

Chanting Zhong is for developing all four spiritual channels. Focus your mind on the Zhong area in the lower abdomen visualizing a golden light ball radiating in the Zhong space.
When you chant Zhong you could have one or more of the following experiences:
- An increase in energy, stamina, vitality, and immunity
- Sudden ability to translate Soul Language (*Soul Language Channel* opening)
- Sudden ability to hear and have a conversation with the Divine and the Soul World (*Direct Soul Communication Channel* opening)
- Sudden ability to see spiritual images (*Third Eye Channel* opening)
- Sudden direct knowing ability (*Direct Knowing Channel* opening)

When you chant *Zhong* you could suddenly forget where you are or what time it is. That is the Zhong condition, emptiness condition, nothingness condition, and Tao condition. Stay in this condition for as long as you can. When you become aware of space and time again, chant *Zhong* again. *Be in the divine and Tao condition for as long as possible.* Read *Wuji Qigong Tai Chi Yin Yang Ball by Chang San-feng, p. 74*
"Listening to your heart by practicing soul communication regularly will improve your health and happiness a thousand fold." - Ricardo B Serrano, Tao Soul Communicator With thanks to Tao Grandmaster Zhi Gang Sha
Breathe less to heal, sleep soundly and do more. – Ricardo B Serrano
I am a Traditional Chinese Medicine practitioner since 1980 with Qigong, Tai Chi and breathing exercises. I have found that incorporating *Buteyko breathing* exercises with physical exercise and other traditional healing arts like Qigong and Tai Chi helped to a greater degree to cure my personal and my clients' health challenges like high blood pressure, panic attacks, snoring, fatigue and eye problems.
The *Buteyko method of breathing* which I have been practicing for a few years is a simple, fast way to cure almost all health problems because of its biochemical, biomechanical and psychological effects in the body-mind connection especially in these post-pandemic stressful times we are all experiencing now. I find that incorporating Buteyko breathing strengthens the immune system because of its normalizing and eventual restoring of lung functions. It's use increases breathing capacity and calms the sympathetic nervous system. It also helps open the airways, improves blood circulation and sends oxygen throughout the body. – Ricardo B Serrano, *Certified Buteyko breathing instructor*
Read *Buteyko Breathing Method*, page 85

Microcosmic Orbit Qigong

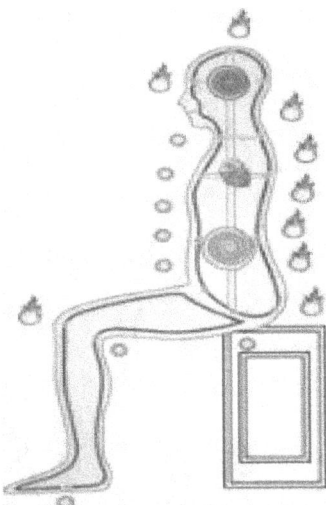

Microcosmic Orbit

This meditative non-moving Microcosmic Orbit Qigong involves the circulation of Qi throughout the body to strengthen both the body and mind to arrive at enlightened consciousness. In this cleansing process, one's being is uplifted and a deeper understanding of life follows. As you are relaxed and quiet, as the qi becomes concentrated, qi can then circulate gently and lightly to benefit the body. This Qigong achieves a purified and focused mind that can become one with the collected qi. If you practice this qigong while understanding its deeper meaning, nothing can afflict you. With accumulated qi, you will experience good health, a good disposition, and a sense of perfect well-being in your life.

CONTEMPLATION

The human body is a flame.
Let the qi calm and stop the flames of desire.
Moving the qi is also moving the mind.
Let the mind balance and harmonize the qi in the body.
The fresh, clean qi can flush out the dirty qi.
Consciously release the dirty qi.
Then the body is left with only clean and clear qi.
As the clean qi fills the body, it takes on the shape of the human form.
Pure qi then permeates every pore in the body.

Microcosmic Orbit Chart with Important Points in the Functional and Governor Channels

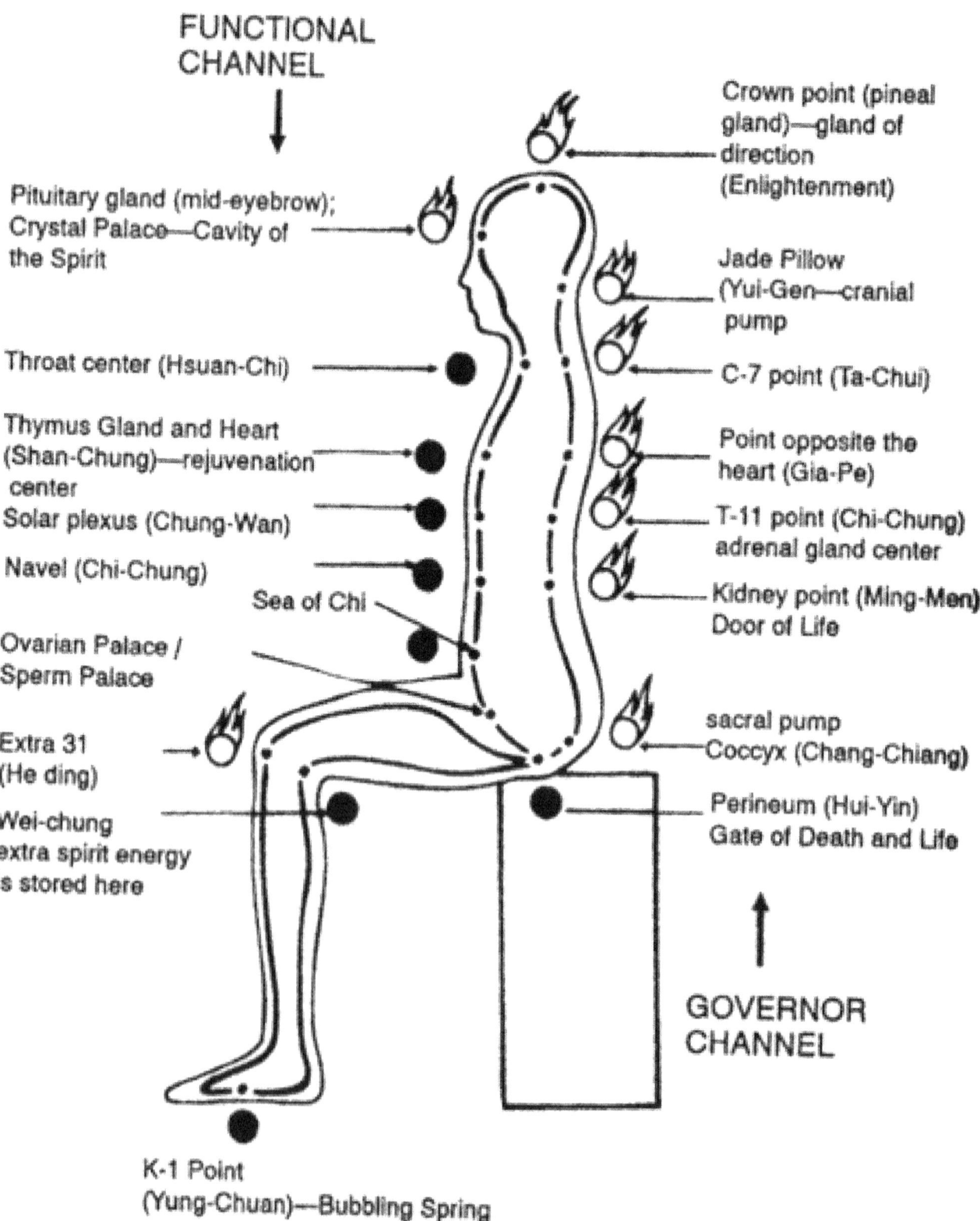

Microcosmic Orbit Chart with Important Points

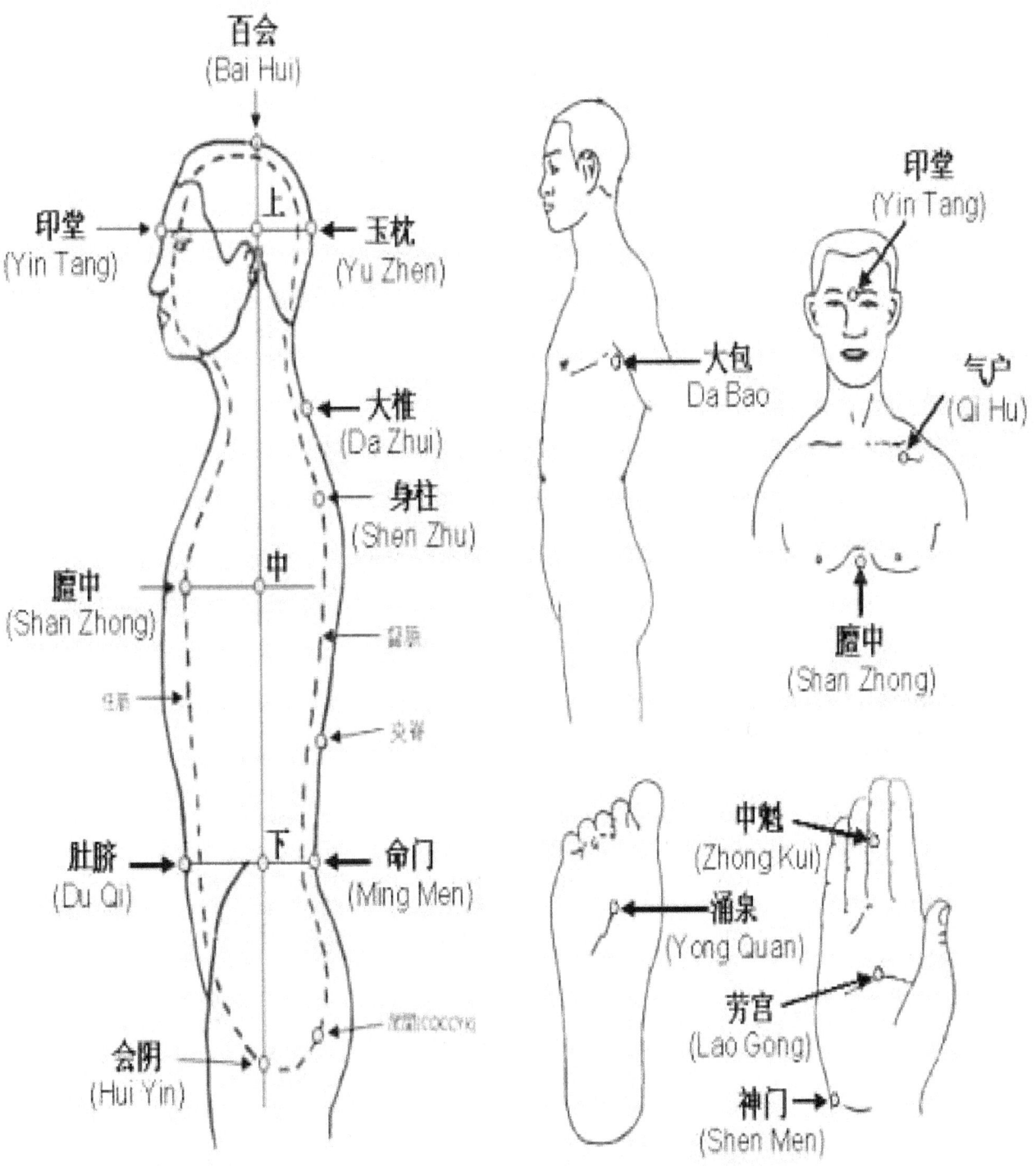

Qi circulation along the back and front channels

Another important technique to be done after Zhongtian Yiqi meditation is called The Microcosmic Orbit Qigong to circulate the kundalini Qi energy along the back and front channels of the body.

This is a classic Taoist Meditation method, with it's roots in India, for circulating and refining Qi via the circuit formed by the 'Governing Channel' from perineum up to head and the 'Conception Channel' from head back down to perineum.

Practicing the Microcosmic Orbit is a key step that enables more advanced practices.

The Practice of the Microcosmic Orbit

1. The first steps are to still the body, calm the mind, and regulate the breath. Sit, stand in Zhan Zhuang or lay on your back, in a quiet place, eyes closed lightly. If you are sitting, you should be upright, with your feet flat on the floor, sitting forward enough so your genitals are off the chair. Advanced practitioners can use many of the different Zhan Zhuang postures.
2. Focus your attention on your Dan Tian (just below your navel and above the Du Qi), and visualize a small ball of energy, *a ball of golden or white light*, bright and pure. Maintain the attention on the Dan Tian until you feel the energy of the ball. This could be heat, vibration, warmth or just a sensation of its presence.
3. Begin abdominal breathing. This breathing method starts when you inhale through your nose and your abdomen expands, not your chest. It is the way babies breathe. Exhale through your slightly opened mouth, keeping your tongue lightly touching your palate just behind your upper front teeth. When you exhale your abdominal muscles contract lightly to help expel air.
4. Inhale and visualize or imagine this small ball of Qi passing down from the Dan Tian, past the Hui Yin, up through the coccyx. Then visualize or imagine the Qi ball rising up to the Ming Men and then to where the ribs meet the spine, then going through this area and right on up to the back of the head, where it joins the neck.
5. Then visualize or imagine this Qi ball in the center of your brain, taking in healing energy through the Bai Hui point on the top of your head.
6. Next, focus your attention on the Yin Tang point between and just above the eyebrows and draw energy into the ball of Qi from this point as the ball passes and goes to the roof of your mouth. This may cause a tingling or throbbing sensation there. This ends your inhalation.
7. You may wish to stay and work with this Qi for a few minutes, before letting Qi sink down through the palate and tongue (which you still have lightly pressed onto your palate), into the throat to the heart (Shan Zhong point). Taking a breath or two while the Qi is in your mouth can help you focus on the ball. This is OK for beginners.
8. Exhale and send the Qi down to your heart (Shan Zhong Point). From the heart, draw it down through the middle Dan Tian at your solar plexus, past your navel, and down into the lower Dan Tian, where energy gathers, mixes, and is reserved for internal circulation. Then begin another cycle.

IMPORTANT NOTES

Once the Qi is circulating, your breath will naturally become fine. This means it is smooth, not ragged or irregular. You can do this meditation from one to dozens of times.

Qi circulation harmonizes and reforms, so that the vital fluids produced by daily life can produce true vitality.

If you have any physical problems or discomforts in a particular section of your body, while doing the orbit, hold the circulation and focus your Qi at the discomforting point and let it pulse there for a while. This will help heal and rejuvenate and improve the Qi flow.

This meditation may also cause the head to rock or the body to tremble, which, some believe, are signs of progress.

If you have high blood pressure and want to use this meditation as part of your treatment, reverse the flow of the orbit, so that your Qi goes up during the inhale and back and down on the exhale.

The Microcosmic Orbit is a good practice for all Qigong students, and can be used before other meditations. You can use a few orbits in both directions during the day, to reduce stress. You can also do this lying down before sleep. Don't do this while driving or operating machinery!

If you have trouble visualizing or imagining Energy, you can think of a golf ball or ping-pong ball. You can even use one hand to trace the flow when you are sitting or standing.

One quick note:
- This meditation (can be simple) with only 2 steps circling the energy with resonance and breath and the other step is connect the tongue to the roof of mouth to connect the energy circuit, and can be done on a busy street corner and people around you don't need to know what your doing and works great in spiritual group because it puts a person in a cocoon of prana (Healing). Energy follows thought!

VERY small NOTE: THIS MEDITATION IS OVER 5000 YEARS OLD

PRIMORDIAL WUJI QIGONG for ENLIGHTENMENT

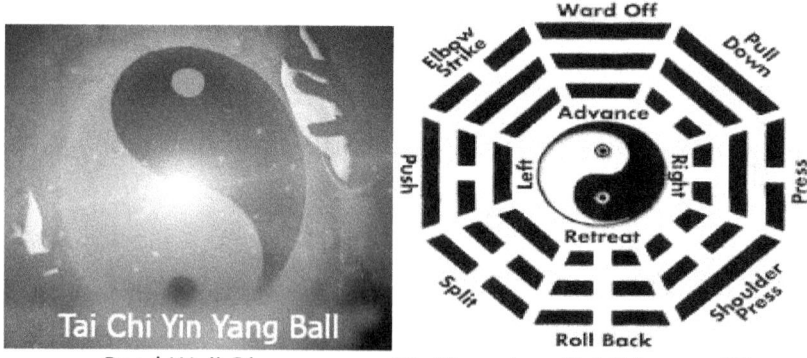

Read *Wuji Qigong*, page 82; *13-posture Tai Chi*, page 95

Practice wuji qigong once a day and no harm will come your way -- Master Zhu Hui

In agreement with the Taoist inner alchemy principle regarding balancing the yin (passive) and yang (active) phases of nature through moving meditation, I have included the Tai Chi for Enlightenment -- *Wuji Qigong* -- to balance the passive sitting meditation, to reconnect the Wu Ji Qigong practitioner with the Taoist immortals -- the Taoist ascended masters -- and enter the Wuji state of original Oneness, the unity or cosmic consciousness. Practicing wuji qigong activates one's lightbody (Merkaba), opens one's heart to unconditional love and heals holographically. Because wu ji qigong grounds spirit into one's body, activates more Qi flow, and births, refines and expands one's energy body -- *immortal or golden light body*, it serves as a ritual communication technique, medium or vehicle between humans and Tao immortals which can ensure success in psychic self-defense, absent and holographic healing, body rejuvenation and age reversal, chakra encoding into the Christ Consciousness grid, balancing chakras, clearing bad habits, thought forms and emotions, ascension process, clairvoyance, abundance consciousness, and love, unity or Cosmic consciousness.

Whole body enlightenment is made possible through Wu Ji Qigong by gathering male (yang)/female (yin) vital organ spirits at the *lower dan tien*; gathering the Sun/Moon essences at the *solar plexus*; gathering yin and yang star essences at the *heart*; and gathering true yin and true yang essences of heaven and earth at the *3rd eye*.

The magical Tai Chi for Enlightenment by Taoist Master Michael Winn is the moving *Cosmic Heart Spiral of Love Wu Ji Qigong form* with *Inner Smile* -- reconnecting one's heart with the cosmic and earth heart through the Qigong 4 earth and heaven spiraling cycles -- that I have adapted with the *Sacred Union* techniques and have been searching for which embodies the "tai chi mind", the living dynamic Sacred Geometry such as the Metatronic Waveform Pattern and the hexagram mantra OM MANI PADME HUM.

Read *Vajrasattva Qigong*, page 80; *13-posture Tai Chi by Master Helen Liang*, page 95

What is *"Tai Chi mind"* in Tao Cosmology?

According to Michael Winn, "The ascended Tao masters are said to hang out in a state of pure openness called wuji. It looks like emptiness, but its not. It is filled with the original Oneness, called in China *Original Breath (Yuan Chi)*. *Wuji* is the Taoist equivalent of the *Godhead*, the direct doorway to the Tao itself, from which *Original Chi* first breathes life into Creation. *Tao* is the undefinable totality of Nature. It embraces non-being as well, so Tao is even beyond our concept of a Creator-God.

Wuji is thus like the Godhead without a God or Goddess sitting in it. It the closest that humans can aspire to returning to the Origin, the formless One source of all life before Creation begins birthing what Lao Tzu calls *"the ten thousand things"*. The Tao Immortals only leave this Oneness state of pure potential if we sincerely call upon them to help us evolve spiritually. They will only meet us if we come halfway. Doing this Tai Chi form - created by a Tao Immortal - acts as a kind of sacred dance, a ritual communication between us humans and the Tao Immortals.

Tai Chi (or "taiji") is a cosmological term. *"Tai Chi mind"* refers to a state of consciousness. Tai chi literally means *"Great Ultimate"*. It has nothing to do with martial arts. It is an enlightenment term, describing the stage where female yin (condensing) chi and male yang (expanding) chi flow in harmony. Tai Chi for Enlightenment helps us to cultivate Original Chi, which is what births all yin and yang chi, and maintains the harmony between them.

Tai Chi is the state of mind that precedes entrance into the higher Wuji state of Original Chi. Thus Tai Chi for Enlightenment is also called *wuji qigong*, meaning *"skill at entering the Supreme Unknown"*. When we practice Tai Chi for Enlightenment, it signals to the Tao Immortals to help us open an effortless tai chi path between our human ego state and the Wuji state of original Oneness.

It cultivates both earth chi, heaven chi, and human heart chi. It immediately activates your Energy Body and begins the process of awakening your Original Spirit."

Tai Chi for Enlightenment (Wu Ji Qigong) as embodiment of the living dynamic Sacred Geometry

According to Michael Winn, "We are going to focus mostly on learning the cycle of earth form today. That has 12 movements in it. Number 12 in Taoist numerology is considered to be one of the numbers of the Earth. There are others as well, but twelve is one of the most important in an earthly cycle. It's related to the 12 meridians in your body, and the 12 hour "chi clock" of their flow cycle. It is related to -- depending upon which calendar you want to use -- the 12 lunar months in the year.

If you get into Sacred Geometry, the Chinese calendar is based on cycles of twelve. It's based on five cycles of twelve, total sixty year cycle, which in Sacred Geometry also forms a dodecahedron (twelve pentagons formed into a sphere). It is considered to be the inner shape of planet earth.

You could basically consider this form to be a mandala. We are creating a moving, geometric mandala. In that sense, it's dynamic Sacred Geometry as well. *It's embodied, living Sacred Geometry. We are basically doing a sacred dance within that mandala.* Our doing the form of that dance, and the energetic pathway that's already been created by previous masters doing this form, combine to empower that pattern. Of course, since this form also embodies the Chinese calendar, we are doing a sacred dance with Time, that is how we accelerate Time itself...

The physical movements are gestures, but they are loaded gestures. Symbolic or ritual gestures in a sense. You are gathering something. It is not the physicality of the movement that matters most. That's one of the things that distinguishes it from martial tai chi, where the physical applications are very present. You are doing martial applications even if you don't know it, so it matters there, every tiny physical detail is crucial.

Here it does not matter. That's why you can stay very relaxed with this form. And it's why people get more chi from doing it. Correction: *its is not that they get more chi -- they activate more chi flow*. The chi is already inside you, always present. You activate it more easily with this form than with tai chi. Because in martial and even health tai chi they are too concentrated about their body and so they shrink down their chi field to the size of their body, and then they become a little tense and too contracted to let it flow easily. They are always concerned, am I doing it right?

But here, we are always constantly expanding our Energy Body. With all of these perfect polarities built into each set of movements. Front and back, left and right, up and down. We're in a continuous looping flow. It's almost like a *Celtic cross*. Have you seen the Celtic cross? Everybody, take your hand and start to make these loops. That's really what a Celtic cross is like. You can go one up and one down, one left and one right. *They are just a series of figure eights, and they are all crossing back in the center.* You can have one go behind you and one go in front of you.

In this form we are making, in the whole movement, the whole dance, a kind of multi-dimensional Celtic cross. That's really what we are doing. And maybe that's one reason it has amazing, calming, and centering effect. Because everything comes back to center, even as it loops out this way and it loops out that way.

As you become more present with this form, your awareness will go more deeply into the movements. It will not just be a movement. It will be your whole energy shifting out. You whole awareness flowing back in. And so you are *slowly achieving integration*. That is what you are doing.

The way it works, is ordinarily your ego consciousness is fragmented. It's very jangled -- one piece is here, one piece is there, and this part of me wants to do that, and this part of me has a desire for this. And this one says I have to go pay my rent. And this one says I need to deal with my husband or my wife. Or my kid or whatever.

These are all these different voices and they are all pulling you in different directions. Naturally, your chi will be scattered. Well, we are gathering those fragments, and looping them all back together. Linking them up, smoothing them out, and taking them back into their natural center. That's essentially what's going on with this form. All those fragments of yourself are being gathered back into inner space, from where you originally projected them out into the world."

"I believe that happiness is what we feel when our biochemicals of emotion, the neuropeptides and their receptors, are open and flowing freely throughout the psychosomatic network, integrating and coordinating our systems, organs, and cells in a smooth and rhythmic movement. Health and happiness are often mentioned in the same breath, and maybe this is why: Physiology and emotions are inseparable. I believe that happiness is our natural state, that bliss is hardwired. Only when our systems get blocked, shut down, and disarrayed do we experience the mood disorders that add up to unhappiness in the extreme. " – Dr. Candace Pert, PhD, *Molecules of Emotion*

What exactly is Tai Chi for Enlightenment?

This secret Tai Chi for Enlightenment form combines tai chi, feng shui, chi kung (qigong), and inner alchemy, a powerful form of Taoist meditation. It is designed to capture the *"subtle breath"* or chi (*"qi"*) flow of Heaven and Earth, and fuse it into the human body. *It gathers chi inward to the core of one's being in graceful beautiful, effortless spirals.*

Tai Chi for Enlightenment gradually dissolves all the physical and karmic layers of tension in both your physical and Energy Body. It ultimately opens up a profound inner space inside your body, where your Original Spirit, the *"face of your soul before you were born"*, can reveal itself. This inner space is called *"wuji"* (Supreme Unknown) - the Primordial space.

The design of the form incorporates every aspect of Tao theory: Yin-Yang body channels, 5 Elements vital organ and seasonal cycles, feng shui (directionology) of the 8 Trigram forces (Pakua), water and fire alchemy, the 10 Heavenly Stems and 12 Branches of the Chinese calendar, body-spirit and microcosm-macrocosm resonance, Taoist sexual-numerology, jing-chi-shen-wu stages of inner alchemy, tai chi body movement principles, Original Chi -Tai Chi -Wuji cosmology. It is truly amazing how much is packed into one tiny little form!

Grandmaster Chang San Feng created Tai Chi for Enlightenment. It has 13 movements: 12 movements of Earth and one movement of Heaven that is done 50 times, ten times in each of the five directions. It was secretly practiced by a lineage of Taoist masters for the last 800 years.

This secret Tai Chi for Enlightenment form was taught to Michael Winn by the 84- year old *Zhu Hui*, a kindly Chinese master with a smile that made your heart melt. He says the form cured his liver cancer and protected him from violent abuse during the Cultural Revolution. He learned it from a 106-year old Taoist Master *Li Tong*, who lived on Wudang Mountain. Zhu Hui was the national tai chi sword champion of China when he was younger, and Master Li Tong took a liking to him. Although the form is designed for Enlightenment, it has many beneficial medical effects. Dr. Zhu Hui had a major clinic in China and used it to treat more than ten types of chronic diseases, especially *heart diseases and high blood pressure, and for people with weak kidneys or chi deficiency.*

To prevent respiratory diseases caused by virus infections, the Qi deficient immune system has to be strengthened by acupuncture, Qigong, Qi-healing, Tao healing hands and herbs with *Buteyko breathing*. Wuji Qigong treats Qi deficiency effectively (with intranasal light therapy). The model of the immune system used in the Chinese herbal and acupuncture systems presents a simple view that has proven quite functional. Whether a contagious or climate-induced condition is interior or exterior depends on the strength of one's immune system, which in turn is related to the concept Wei Qi or protective Qi. When the protective Qi is strong, diseases from viruses and weather influences entering the body are completely warded off; if it is less strong, diseases may enter onto an exterior level and bring about a cold, flu, or other exterior condition; if it is very deficient, disease factors may penetrate to interior levels, more profoundly affecting the functioning of internal organs. See Intranasal Light Therapy, pages 98, 100 and 102

*Nothing is permanent, even the coronavirus. Become centered with meditation
and peace will come.* – Acharya Ricardo B Serrano

In that great goddess there is the great joy (of the conjunction of the *mantra so'ham*) which is like a jnana or sacrifice (of vimarsha or I-consciousness). Pursuing it and resting in it (i.e. in the joy of the *mantra*), one becomes identified with the great goddess and thus (through her) one attains to bhairava. See page 57

The cause of health problems essentially lies in a *lack* of energy and information in one part of the energy system that corresponds to an *overactivity* in other parts. The principle of this qigong is that you use the excess energy from the system to nurture the deficient system. Read *One Hand Near, One Hand Far*, page 65

Importance of Smiling and the mantra OM Mani Padme Hum or OM NAMAH SHIVAYA in Tai Chi

There is one other skill that will greatly speed your exciting journey to Enlightenment. It's the secret of Taoist inner soul alchemy, a simple practice called the Inner Smile. It assures that your innermost heart is present every moment of your daily life, and especially during your practice of Tai Chi for Enlightenment. It magically opens your chi flow. One of my many masters taught me, *"If you smile while practicing tai chi, your chi is ten times more powerful!"*

I find that enclosing the mantra *OM MANI PADME HUM* or OM NAMAH SHIVAYA while intoning it within the hologram of love Omkabah while doing Qigong forms such as Microcosmic Orbit Qigong, Eight Extraordinary Vessels Qigong, and especially Wu Ji Qigong exponentially activates much more Qi life force within the practitioner making ascension (expansion of consciousness), healing and whole body enlightenment attainable. *Weng Mani Ba Ma Hong* mantra can also be used to activate *Chong Mai* (central channel).

A beautiful lotus flower is likened to an enlightened being rooted to mother earth.
- Acharya Ricardo B Serrano

I would also recommend that you practice Wuji Yuan Gong to continuously activate the opening of your heart to unconditional love (Sheng Zhen) – a powerful ritual communication between men, the immortals and Kundalini Shakti (mother earth). See Te and Mu: Great Mother, pages 52 - 53

*Without meditation, your Qigong suffers
Without Qigong, your meditation suffers*

"The emotions are a key element in self-care because they allow us to enter into the body mind's conversation. By getting in touch with our emotions, both by listening to them and by directing them through the psychosomatic network, we gain access to the healing wisdom that is everyone's natural biological right.

And how do we do this? First by acknowledging and claiming all our feelings, not just the so- called positive ones. Anger, grief, fear – these emotional experiences are not negative in themselves; in fact, they are vital for survival. We need anger to define boundaries, grief to deal with our losses, and fear to protect ourselves from danger. It's only when these feelings are denied, so that they cannot be easily and rapidly processed through the system and released, that the situation becomes toxic. And the more we deny them, the greater the ultimate toxicity, which often takes the form of an explosive release of pent-up emotion. That's when emotion can become damaging to both oneself and others, because its expression becomes overwhelming, sometimes even violent.

So my advice is to express all of your feelings, regardless of whether you think they are acceptable, and then let them go. Buddhists understand this when they talk about nongrasping, or nonattachment to experience. By letting all emotions have their natural release, the "bad" ones are transformed to "good" ones, and in Buddhist terms, we are then liberated from suffering. When your emotions are moving and your chemicals flowing, you will experience feelings of freedom, hopefulness, joy, because you are in a healthy, "whole" state. The goal is to keep information flowing, feedback systems working, and natural balance maintained, all of which we can help to achieve by a conscious decision to enter into the body mind's conversation."
– Dr. Candace Pert, PhD *Molecules of Emotion*

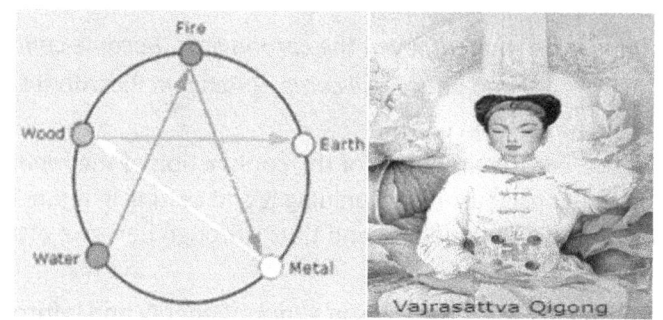

Five Element Organ Correspondences

Elements	Fire	Metal	Earth	Water	Wood
Organs	Heart	Lungs	Spleen	Kidneys	Liver
Color	Red	White	Yellow	Blue	Green
Planets	Mars	Venus	Saturn	Mercury	Jupiter
Directions	South	West	Center	North	East
+ Emotions	Love	Courage	Openness	Gentleness	Kindness
- Emotions	Hate	Sadness	Worry	Fear	Anger
Animals	Pheasant	White Tiger	Phoenix	Blue Tortoise	Green Dragon
Seasons	Summer	Autumn	Indian Summer	Winter	Spring
Cranium	Frontal	L. Parietal	Sphenoid	Occipital	R. Parietal

FOOTNOTES:
Heaven (universal energy) is related to 10 heavenly stems and 5 elements, and upper tan tien (ni-wuan); Man (Cosmic energy) is related to 9 stars and 8 forces (pakua), and middle tan tien (heart); and Earth energy is related to 12 branches and 12 meridians, and lower dantian.

Ten Heavenly Stems correspond to the yin and yang poles of each of the five elements (fire, earth, metal, water and wood). The ten heavenly stems are often related with the planets and the five palaces in the star world. The ten heavenly stems have a high-frequency energy, and are related both to cosmic law and to universal energy.

Twelve Earthly Branches correspond to the twelve animals of the Chinese zodiac, are in relationship with the earthly forces and also the twelve acupuncture meridians. The twelve earthly branches have a lower frequency and are related to the earth energy and surroundings of the earth in the twelve different directions, and to the twelve sections of the earth's rotation field projected onto the star world.

Water and Fire Alchemy On the inbreath draw the silver/white moonlight into the sacrum/sexual center (blue) and at the same time draw the golden/ yellow sunlight into the third eye/heart center (red). On the outbreath condense these two energies in the central point behind the navel (dantian). Push the blue/ silver/ white energy up and the red/ golden/ yellow energy down. Keep drawing these energies in until you feel a clear connection.

On the inbreath picture Mars as a red ball above the frontal bone. Connect Mars frontal bone and heart. Picture Mercury as a blue ball above the occipital bone. Connect Mercury and kidneys. On the outbreath condense these two energies in the central point behind the navel.

The sun/moon meditation and to a lesser extent the Mars/Mercury meditation can help people who have problems integrating their experiences of the past and balancing their concerns for the future. Today many people are stuck in past experiences. These experiences have an emotional charge and are related to pain that may be constantly denied or intellectually repressed. For these people, the sun connection will bring relief, more vision of the future, and another view of the past. Others strive only for future experiences and run away from themselves constantly. The moon/Mercury meditations will bring them closer to where they come from and to the forces and influences that have shaped their emotional body.

 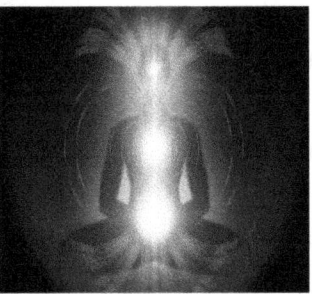

The 3 *dantiens* (ball of light) in the 3 *San Jiao* - upper dantien (head), middle dantien (heart) and lower dantien (lower abdomen) can be activated by chanting mantra *Weng* (red) *Ar* (white) *Hong* (blue). It is best combined with mantra *Weng Mani Ba Ma Hong* to activate *Chong Mai* in *Vajrasattva Qigong* practice, see photo, p.80 for improving the circulation of Qi and blood and strengthening Qi in the *lower dantian and immune system*.

PRIMORDIAL CHI KUNG PROCEDURE
(Wu Ji Qigong)
Taught to me by
Michael Winn

Start facing EAST, the direction of sunrise & new beginnings. Open your heart to change. Inwardly smile, tone, or call to the Beings of All Directions, focusing on the 4 directions & 3 realms of Heaven center above/ Earth center below/ Human center within. Hold clear intention to return to your core being, to hold the center in outer life, and balance all perceptions arising in the present moment.

Open yourself to being in "wu ji", the "supreme unknown", the primordial space. It's the Origin, Godhead, Primal Mother at the center of all sacred space. Ask to create your life from this center; to accept its power of unconditional acceptance to solve any problem & complete your life.

1st EARTH CYCLE: Flow of 12 Body Meridians (12 hour chi clock)
1. Breath (chi) of Earth Rises. *Arms raise to chest level (palms down).*
Breath of Heaven Descends. *Arms sink down. Form small chi ball, R. palm below.*

2. Yin/Yang separates to honor Yin. *Look (3rd eye) at palm as R. arm, weight sweeps R. Press L. palm face down, by left leg.*

3. Yin/Yang separates to honor Yang. *Look left (3rd eye) at palm as L. arm, weight sweeps L., R. palm presses to right.*

4. Circulate chi in orbit. *Palms face each other, circle up from belly to crown, out & down to perineum, back up to heart, arms extend out.*

5. Heart opens, time flows to right (manifest). *Rotate chest level chi ball to R.*

6. Heart opens, time flows to the left (unmanifest). *Rotate large chi ball to L.*

7. Heart opens, time flows to right (manifest). *Rotate large chi ball to R.*

8. Gather chi from East. *R. hand drops below, rotate chi ball inward, <u>top to bottom.</u>*

9. Gather chi from North. *Pivot left: weight on R. foot, turn on L. heel to L., R. foot steps in, faces north. Rotate chi ball inward, <u>hands on sides</u> (alternating L & R)*

10. Gather chi from West. Pivot left, rotate chi ball inward, <u>top to bottom.</u>

11. Gather chi from South. Pivot left, rotate chi ball inward, hands on sides. THIS 2ND HANDS ON SIDES MOVEMENT IS CUE FOR END OF EARTH CYCLE.

13. Gather chi from Center. Half squat, keeping back straight. Both arms scoop up chi ball below, circle up to 3rd eye, "swallow" it down center line of body to dan tien (1.5" below navel). Breathe 3x into chi ball inside ming men (between kidneys), feel & visualize it as golden light expanding & condensing.

<u>1st HEAVEN CYCLE</u>: Gather Female (yin) and Male (yang) Vital Organ Spirits

<u>1.</u> *<u>After Earth, always quarter turn to begin Heaven cycle.</u>*
Turn from South to East. BEFORE YOU TURN, REMEMBER WHAT YOU ARE LOOKING AT. This will be your CUE for the final direction of the upcoming Heaven cycle.
  Pivot left, right arm sweeps high & wide as R. foot steps to east.
  Gather chi from southeast corner as you turn from south to east.

<u>2.</u> Heaven & Earth Separate. *Form chi ball at navel; eyes follow R. hand as it rises to Heaven. Left hand presses down to earth.*

<u>3.</u> Gather heavenly Yin <u>*inner female*</u> and Yang <u>*inner male*</u> essence into the body.
5x each hand = 10x. (count with fingers). Full wt. Shift to L. foot as R. hand gathers chi into left side of body. L hand gathers chi into channels on right side of body.

<u>4.</u> Turn to North. *Gather chi of northeast as you turn. Repeat 10x.*

<u>5.</u> Turn to West. *Gather chi of northwest as you turn. Repeat 10x.*

<u>6.</u> Turn to South. *Gather chi of southwest as you turn. Repeat 10x.*

<u>7.</u> Stir the Cauldron 9x, Gather Alchemical Essence of the Center direction.
R palm faces navel, stir circling up R, down L. (full wt.) v.v. Scoop up below,
Gather down center line to lower dan tien. Breathe into chi ball 3x in mingmen

2nd EARTH CYCLE: Flow of 12 Planetary Meridians (ley lines; 12 lunar months)
1. *After heaven, face forward,* begin Earth cycle facing South.
2. Turn (left) to East, North & finish West. Pivot left to South to begin Heaven cycle.

2nd HEAVEN CYCLE: Gather Sun and Moon Essence
1. Start new Heaven cycle (10x) facing South. *Turn East, North, finish West.*
2. Stir Cauldron, gather essence to center. *Hands pause at solar plexus, breathe 3x. Hands move chi ball down to lower dan tien.*

3rd EARTH CYCLE: Flow of 12 houses of zodiac (solar system rotates)
1. *After Heaven, face forward,* begin Earth cycle facing North.
2. Turn (left) to East, & finish North. Pivot left to West to begin Heaven cycle.

3rd HEAVEN CYCLE: Gather Yin & Yang Star Essences
1. Start new Heaven cycle (10x) facing West. *Turn South, East, finish North.*
2. Hands pause at heart, breathe 3x. Hands move chi ball down to lower dan tien.

4th EARTH CYCLE: Flow of prenatal chi for rebirthing spiritual embryo.
1. *After Heaven,* begin Earth cycle facing North.
2. Turn (left) to West, South & finish East. Pivot left to North to begin Heaven cycle.

4th HEAVEN CYCLE: Gather True Yin and True Yang essences of Heaven & Earth
1. Start new Heaven cycle (10x) facing North. *Turn West, South & finish East.*
2. Stir Cauldron, gather essence to center. *Hands pause at 3rd eye, breathe 3x. Hands move chi ball down to lower dan tien.*

NOTE: To assist your Wuji Qigong practice, please watch the Primordial Wuji Qigong movie rendered by me showing the 1st Earth Cycle & 1st Heavenly Cycle at http://vimeo.com/631197872

6-3-6-3 BALANCING BREATHING EXERCISE

- Curl the tip of your tongue up your palate.
- To control the airflow through your nostrils, use the right middle finger or index finger to close the left nostril and the right thumb to close the right nostril.
- With your left nostril closed, inhale through the right nostril for six counts.
- Hold your breath for three counts.
- Close the right nostril and exhale through the left nostril for six counts.
- Hold for three counts.
- Inhale through the left nostril for six counts.
- Hold for three counts.
- Close the left nostril and exhale through the right nostril for six counts. This is one cycle. Do this for seven cycles.

It is important to do the physical Qigong exercises and the balancing breathing technique before doing the Meditation on the Soul. These will:
1. Prepare the physical body and energy body for the greater amount of subtle energy that will be generated during the meditation; and
2. Calm the mind so that the Meditation on the Soul can be done properly.

What are the benefits of practicing the balancing breathing technique?

Normally, one side of the brain has more energy. Likewise, one side of the body is usually stronger than the other side. The balancing breathing technique therefore balances the energy level of the right and left sides of the brain, and that of the right and left sides of the body. It also cleanses and energizes the whole energy body, including the chakras and the energy channels.

Buteyko Breathing Method: *The perfect man is breathing as if he is not breathing. – Lao Tzu*

Three principles sum up the practice: (1) nasal breathing; (2) a return to normal breathing if there is a problem; and (3) a Control Pause of up to 15-25 seconds and a Maximum Pause of 40 seconds. The Control Pause measures how long the breath can be held after exhaling.

The Buteyko method includes seven exercises with slight variations. The goal of the practice is to breathe through the nose 24 hours a day with the tongue resting on the roof of the mouth. This helps to open the airways, improves blood circulation, and sends oxygen throughout the body. Because mouth breathing is so common, beginners may feel they are not getting enough air at first, but the feeling goes away with practice.

Exercise 1 clears nasal congestion and makes it easier to breathe through the nose.
Exercise 2 uses hand positions and blocked nostril breathing to increase the volume of inhaled air.
Exercise 3 engages belly breathing while walking.
Exercise 4 combines breath holds and walking to lengthen the time the breath can be held.
Exercise 5 makes breathing easier for adults and children with anxiety, asthma, or panic attacks.
Exercise 6 uses short, repetitive breath holds.
Exercise 7 induces relaxation with slow breathing.

Students of the Buteyko method learn to combine various exercises to meet specific needs. For example, someone with asthma or anxiety may practice exercises 5 and 7 to increase breathing capacity and calm the sympathetic nervous system.

To open soul communication channels, read *Tao Immortal Way Breathing*, page 68; *Mantra for Third Eye*, page 86; *Tao Healing Hands*, page 88; *Four spiritual channels*, page 92; Soul language mantra *San San Jiu Liu Ba Yao Wu* in my book *Six healing Qigong sounds with Mantras. You become what you chant. – Master Sha*

Mantra *Ling yao chi chi chi, Jiu ling ba, Ling yao chi chi chi, Jiu er er si si* are for opening one's third eye and for developing mind intelligence. See mantras for left, right brain, corpus callosum, below.

The Caduceus symbolizes the three energy channels. The rod or staff stands for the central channel or the sushumna nadi in Sanskrit. The two snakes symbolize two additional energy channels. One energy channel starts from the center at the base of the central meridian, moves to the left, spirals upward and passes to the right side of the head, ending on the crown; from the crown, an energy channel extends down to the right nostril. This energy channel is called pingala nadi, and it is a yang meridian; its energy is warm. The other energy channel from the center at the base of the central meridian moves to the right, spirals upward, passes to the left side of the head, ends on the crown, and extends down to the left nostril. This is called the ida nadi. It is a yin meridian and has cooling energy.

- On top of the staff is a small cone that symbolizes the pineal gland, where the blue pearl or the seed of consciousness is located. The wings at the top symbolize the ability of the consciousness to leave the body.

- The balancing breathing technique facilitates cleansing, energizing and balancing of the right (pingala), left (ida) and central channels (sushumna). By doing this breathing exercise, these three channels become clean. It prepares the awakening of the KUNDALINI energy with much less obstructions so that it can go up smoothly without pain. Why must the kundalini energy be awakened? To enable the brain to register the spiritual experiences of meditation. Without the kundalini energy, the brain does not have the capacity to register spiritual stimuli.

- When you practice balancing breathing, do not overdo it. It is advisable to practice for five to seven cycles per session, with a maximum of three sessions per day. You have to observe whether your body can handle the energy. If not, practice the balancing breathing technique for only two sessions per day. In the event that your body still cannot handle the energy, reduce the practice to one session per day. It is definitely advisable not to do too many of this breathing technique. The adverse effects may not be seen immediately, but only after a few days. Overdoing the balancing breathing may lead to kundalini syndrome that may manifest as adverse physical and psychological effects. Kundalini syndrome is difficult to treat, unless one is lucky enough to meet an experienced and powerful energy healer. Chant *Ling yao chi chi chi, Jiu ling ba, Ling yao chi chi chi, Jiu er er si si* 7x or more.

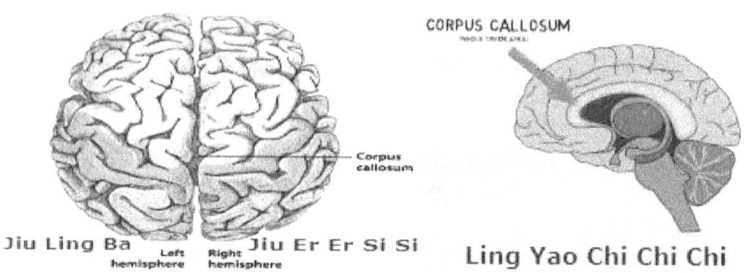

Meditation on the Soul to Realize your Buddha Nature

Read *Vajrasattva Qigong*, pages 80, 81

Do the 6-3-6-3 balancing breathing exercise. Touch lightly the tip of your tongue to your upper palate. Do the Hara (lower dantian) breathing for 3-5 minutes. Concentrate on the pineal gland in the center of the head for a minute. Visualize a dazzling ball of golden light on top of your head and simultaneously chant mentally the word AUM (Ah-omm--), or OM (Ommmmmm). Concentrate on the intervals or gaps (moments of stillness) between AUMs or OMs, while maintaining your concentration on the ball of golden light. Do this for about 5 to 10 minutes. When you can fully concentrate on the golden ball of light and on the intervals between the AUMS or OMs, you will experience an inner explosion of light and expansion of consciousness.

During meditation some may see the blue light or experience inner explosion. Others may experience travelling in all directions, while some may see a tunnel of light or travel inside the tunnel of light. Some people like whirling or exploding, just flow with the inner experience.

Each person is different. Some are spiritually old, while others are still young. Some have been practicing meditation in many incarnations. Just practice regularly and in one or two years' time, most of you should have some inner experience.

Please release excess energy by blessing the earth through your hands with light, loving-kindness, peace, and prosperity for several minutes until your body has normalized. Release excess energy by rooting to Mother Earth. Gently bless the earth either through the feet or through the base of your spine. Also circulate the Qi along the microcosmic orbit to distribute the Qi along the back and front channels.

- The Meditation on the Soul and other meditation techniques of *Maitreya (Shiva) Shen Gong* or *Vajrasatva Qigong* allow you to accelerate the Union of your incarnated soul (often described as the personality, lower self or Buddha Nature) with your Higher Soul (Higher Self). This phenomenon is known as "Soul-Realization", "Enlightenment" or "Self-Realization
- The Higher Soul is a seed of God's Divinity within all of us. Through the Higher Soul, we are made in the Image of God!
- Being One with our Higher Soul, we become One with the "I AM", the Christ, the Buddha (Maitreya), The Shiva, the Krishna Nature within all of us.
- The development of the Buddha Nature can be accelerated by practicing the five virtues, doing service, having proper relationships with other people and with Mother Nature, and through the regular practice of meditation and Maitreya (Shiva) Shen Gong, *13 Tai Chi form*, *Wuji Qigong* or *Vajrasattva Qigong with mantra*.

The Five Virtues are:
- Loving-Kindness and Non-injury
- Generosity and Non-stealing
- Accurate Perception, Correct Expression and Non-falsehood
- Moderation and Non-excessiveness
- Constancy of Aim and Effort, and Non-laziness

Warning

- The energy generated by the Meditation on the Soul is very potent. This will tend to magnify or worsen major psychological problems or physical ailments. If you have any of these conditions, avoid practicing Meditation on the Soul everyday. Do it just once a week. The rest of the week, you may do Maitreya (Shiva) Shen Gong or Meditation on Twin Hearts without the Meditation on the Soul, which can be used for self-healing.
- Pregnant women should be careful in doing Meditation on the Soul, since the energy generated by this meditation is rather potent. Should they experience any pain or discomfort, they should stop the meditation immediately. Pregnant women with a history of miscarriage should avoid doing this meditation.
- Exempted from the rule of avoiding regular practice of Meditation on the Soul are terminal cases. It is advisable for terminally ill patients to do Meditation on the Soul to prepare themselves for death as an opportunity for spiritual liberation. Their stay in the physical body will be partially shortened, therefore, their sufferings will be shortened.

* Meditations for Soul Realization by Master Choa Kok Sui, 2000.

Heal the soul first; then healing of the mind and body will follow. – Master Sha

Soul power is the power of the 21st century. It is the miraculous power we all have. Knowing, developing, and using our soul power will take each one of us and all of humanity to a higher level of existence. The significance of the soul's wisdom and power is beyond our comprehension. We wish that you will develop your soul power and fulfill your highest life purpose.
- Dr. Master Zhi Gang Sha, for more info, read *Six healing Qigong sounds with Mantras* book

Tao Healing Hands   *You have the power to heal and transform yourself.*

Everything has a vibrational field that contains information, energy, and matter. According to Dr. and Master Sha, creator of Tao Hands and co-founder of Tao Science with quantum physicist, Dr. Rulin Xiu, what science calls information (or message) is the same as soul or spirit. It is this very aspect of our being that leads our lives. The positive information we carry in our soul is aligned with our true essence, like the Tao qualities of love, forgiveness, and compassion. The negative information we carry in our soul is associated with our challenges, such as unbalanced emotions, negative thinking, health challenges and more. Tao Hands carry the high frequency and positive information of Tao and the Tao qualities of unconditional love, light, forgiveness, and compassion as shown by the *Soul Light era universal service hand position* photo. Tao Hands has the power to transform the negative information at the root of our many challenges. This could happen instantly or little by little. In this way, Tao Hands can help restore balance and harmony and support progress toward better health and happiness. Tao Hands remove soul, mind and body blockages. Tao Hands have the power to boost energy, stamina, vitality, and immunity of all life. All life includes health, relationships, finances, intelligence and every aspect of life. Tao Hands open spiritual channels and carry divine frequency and vibration, love, forgiveness, compassion and light.

WHAT IS MEDITATION ON TWIN HEARTS?

Meditation on Twin hearts is based on the principle that some of the major chakras are entry points or gateways to certain levels or horizons of consciousness. To achieve illumination or Cosmic consciousness, it is necessary to sufficiently activate the Crown chakra. But this can be done only when the Heart chakra is sufficiently activated. The Twin Hearts thus refer to the Heart and Crown chakras.

The Heart chakra is an energy center in front of a person's chest. It is the energy counterpart of the physical heart. The Heart chakra is the center for compassion, joy, affection, consideration, mercy, and other refined emotions.

The Heart chakra is a replica, or twin of the Crown chakra. When you look at the Heart chakra, it has twelve petals, similar to the twelve petals which form the inner core of the Crown chakra. The Crown chakra, on the other hand, is the center of illumination, or divine love, or oneness with all. It is situated on top of a person's head, providing energy for the brain and the glands therein. When the Crown chakra is sufficiently activated, its inner core of twelve petals unfurl, open and turn upward like a golden cup, golden crown, golden lotus, or golden flower, to receive spiritual energy which is distributed to other parts of the body.

When the Crown chakra is highly activated, a halo is produced around the head. During meditation, the Crown chakra rotates so fast it appears as a brilliant flame of light on top of one's head.

The Twin Hearts Meditation was first introduced in Master Choa Kok Sui's book, the Ancient Science and Art of Pranic Healing (1987). Since the Meditation is a powerful tool in bringing about world peace, Master Choa has granted permission to disseminate, reprint, copy, and reproduce the Meditation with proper acknowledgement.

"But with the knowledge of the body wide psychosomatic network, I was beginning to think of disease-related stress in terms of an information overload, a situation in which the mind-body network is so taxed by unprocessed sensory input in the form of suppressed trauma or undigested emotions that it has become bogged down and cannot flow freely, sometimes even working against itself, at cross-purposes. When stress prevents the molecules of emotion from flowing freely where needed, the largely autonomic processes that are regulated by peptide flow, such as breathing, blood flow, immunity, digestion, and elimination, collapse down to a few simple feedback loop and upset the normal healing response. Meditation, by allowing long-buried thoughts and feelings to surface, is a way of getting the peptides flowing again, returning the body, and the emotions, to health " – Dr. Candace Pert, PhD, *Molecules of Emotion*

What Happens During The Meditation on Twin Hearts?

When a person does Meditation on Twin Hearts, divine energy flows down to the practitioner; filling him with Divine Light, Love and Power. The practitioner becomes a channel of this Divine energy.

Spiritual aspirants who have practiced this meditation for quite sometime may experience being enveloped by dazzling, sometimes blinding light. In addition, practitioners may experience divine ecstasy and bliss, and a feeling of oneness with all creation. This has been a common experience among advanced yogis and saints of all religions, and can be verified through their holy scriptures.

This blinding, brilliant, and dazzling light is known as Heaven Ki in Taoist yoga, or the pillar of light in ancient Jewish Kabbalah traditions. To the Indian yogis and saints, they call this pillar of light, the Antakharana, or spiritual bridge of light. The Christians refer to it as the descent of the Holy Spirit, symbolized by a pillar of light with a descending white dove. The white dove represents the coming down of divine energy. The descent of the divine energy causes the temporary expansion of the practitioner's major chakras and inner aura. But if this meditation is practiced daily for a year, then the expansion may become permanent.

Benefits From The Meditation

When people practice the Meditation on Twin Hearts daily or regularly, their major chakras and auras will increase in size, making their energy bodies more dynamic and stronger. With bigger chakras and inner aura, they can become more powerful healers and can heal most minor ailments very quickly and almost instantaneously. Having a powerful and dynamic energy body not only enhances one's healing powers but also increases one's effectivity and productivity at work. People who have magnetic personalities or great charisma usually have bigger chakras and inner auras than ordinary people, and they tend to have a stronger influence over most people. Furthermore, a person who regularly meditates becomes more intuitive and intelligent. when faced with a problem, he will have the increased ability to see directly through the problem and find the right or proper solutions. Those who intend to practice regularly the Meditation on Twin Hearts, however, should practice self-purification or character-building through daily reflection so their positive characteristics will be magnified or activated.

The Meditation on Twin Hearts Procedure

The Meditation on Twin Hearts is a form of world service. By blessing the earth with loving-kindness, you fill the world with positive spiritual energies. The blessings can be directed to organizations, specific countries, or group of nations. The potency of the blessings is increased many times when done by a group of persons. Another way of blessing the earth with loving-kindness is by daily radio broadcast at an appropriate time with some or most of the listeners participating in the meditation process. When practiced by a large number of people, the meditation miraculously heal the earth; thereby making it more harmonious and peaceful.

WARNING: The following are not allowed to practice the Meditation on Twin Hearts: (1) those below 18 years of age; (2) those with heart trouble, hypertension, glaucoma and severe kidney ailments; and (3) pregnant women. Doing this meditation can have adverse effects to the people with the preceding conditions. People with the above qualifications who insist on practicing the meditation do so at their own risks.

1. Cleansing Exercise. Cleanse the etheric body by doing simple physical exercises for about five to ten minutes. During the exercise, light grayish matter, or used-up prana, is expelled from the etheric body. Physical exercises also minimize possible pranic congestion since the Meditation generates a lot of subtle energies in the body.

2. Invoke for Divine Blessings. The Invocation is important to one's protection, help and guidance. Without the invocation, the practice of any advanced meditational technique can be dangerous.

3. Activating the Heart Chakra. Press the center of your chest (heart area) with your finger for a few seconds. Then concentrate on the front heart chakra and bless the whole world with loving-kindness. The blessing should not be done mechanically. When blessing the entire earth, visualize it as a small ball in front of you, being filled with dazzling bluish pink light. During the blessing with the Prayer of St. Francis of Assisi, visualize people smiling and filled with joy, faith, hope, and peace. Visualize enemies reconciling, embracing and forgiving each other. You should also personally feel joy, happiness, and peace filling your entire being while blessing the earth. Do not direct this blessing to infants, children or individuals because they might be overwhelmed by the intense energy generated by this meditation.

4. Activating the Crown Chakra. Press the top of your head for a few seconds. Then bless the planet earth with loving-kindness from the Crown chakra. Feel the same positive energies you evoked in step 3. Visualize brilliant white light from your Crown chakra blessing the entire earth.

5. Blessing with both Crown and Heart Chakras. Bless the earth simultaneously from both the Crown and Heart chakras with golden light. This will align the two chakras and make the blessing more potent. Feel the same positive energies you evoked in step 3 and 4.

6. Achieving Illumination. For illumination (expansion of conscious-ness), visualize a point of dazzling white light on top of your head and simultaneously chant mentally the word AUM (Ah-omm--), or Amen (Ah-mennn--). Concentrate on the intervals or gaps (moments of silence) between the AUMs of Ammens, while maintaining your concentration on the point of light. Do this for about 10 to 15 minutes. When you can fully concentrate simultaneously on the point of light and on the intervals between the AUMs, you will experience an inner explosion of light.

7. Releasing Excess Energy. After meditation, it is important to release all excess energy by blessing the earth through your hands, with light, loving-kindness, peace, and prosperity for several minutes until you feel your body has normalized. Continue blessing if you still feel congested, otherwise the excess energy may cause headaches and chest pains. The physical body may also deteriorate in the long run if there is too much energy in the etheric body.

IMPORTANT NOTE by Ricardo B Serrano, R.Ac.: Please do the *Hara (Lower Dantian) Breathing* for 3-5 minutes before and after doing the Meditation on Twin Hearts and Meditation on the Soul. Touch your upper palate with the tip of your tongue throughout the Meditation on Twin Hearts and Meditation on the Soul Procedure. Do the *Microcosmic Orbit Qigong* after you finished the Meditation on Twin Hearts and Meditation on the Soul to circulate the kundalini energy accumulated in your *Hara (Lower Dantian)*, and cultivate the Three Treasures Jing, Qi and Shen.

To avoid self-induced energetic psychosis, focusing on the Lower Dantian develop familiarity with remaining rooted by gathering the body's Qi and strengthening the foundation of the body's energy. It is necessary to have all Three Dantians - Lower, Middle, and Upper Dantian (three hearts) - balanced for a more safer and effective perceptions. Practice Three Hearts Meditation to activate and balance dantiens.

Meditation on Three Hearts feels more peaceful and grounding than Twin Hearts meditation. Read Meditation on Three Hearts, page 70 in Six healing Qigong sounds with Mantras book.

Apply Tao healing hands to open all Four spiritual channels:

- *Soul Language Channel* - starts at the Hui Yin acupoint. It flows **straight up** through the seven soul houses in the center of the body to the top of the head and the Bai Hui acupoint. From there it flows down in front of the spinal column back to the Hui Yin acupoint.
- *Direct Soul Communication Channel* – starts in the Zhong, then to message center (heart) and ends in the brain.
- *Third Eye Channel* - starts in the kundalini. The energy of kundalini flows to the tail bone (Wei Lu) area to the spinal cord. From there it flows up through the spinal cord to the brain, where it ends at the Third Eye (pineal gland).
- *Direct Knowing Channel* - starts in the heart and ends in the Zhong area.

Read *Tao Immortal Way Breathing*, page 68; *Microcosmic Orbit Chart points*, page 70; *Three Dantiens*, page 81; *Primordial Wuji Tai Chi Qigong*, page 82; *Mantra for opening Third Eye*, page 86; *Soul Power* and *Tao Healing Hands*, page 88; *Love and Forgiveness* with Soul Song *Love Peace and Harmony* mantra, page 93

Prayer of St. Francis of Assisi

Lord, make me an instrument of peace
Where there is hatred, let me sow love
injury, pardon
error, truth
doubt, faith
despair, hope
discord, unity
sadness, joy
darkness, light

Divine Master, grant that I might not so much seek to be consoled,
as to console to be understood, as to understand to be loved, as to love
for it is in giving that we receive, it is in pardoning that we are pardoned
And it is dying of this ego and recognizing the Christ consciousness within us that we are born to eternal life.

Soul Song *Love Peace and Harmony* is chanted with *Meditation on the Soul* and *Three Hearts*.
Lu La Lu La Li. Lu La Lu La La Li. Lu La Lu La Li Lu La. Lu La Li Lu La. Lu La Li Lu La.
I love my heart and soul. I love all humanity. Join hearts and souls together.
Love, peace and harmony. Love, peace and harmony.

Love melts all blockages and transforms all life. Love yourself - you have the power to heal yourself. Forgiveness brings inner joy and inner peace. Forgiveness is a golden key to living a healthy happy life. – Master Sha

The following articles *Why Practice Tibetan Shamanic Qigong (Qi Dao)? Every Disease is the Outcome of Stress, Whole Disease Approach* and *Quotations from Molecules of Emotion book* will elaborate on the effect of emotional stress as the main cause of disease, and list strategies to release blocked emotions.

"It is my belief that this mysterious energy (Qi) is actually the free flow of information carried by the biochemicals of emotion, the neuropeptides and their receptors.

When stored or blocked emotions are released through touch or other physical methods, there is a clearing of our internal pathways, which we experience as energy. Free of western dualism that insists on disanimated flesh, healers from various Eastern and alternative modalities can literally see the mind in the body, where it does indeed exist, and are adepts at techniques that can get it unstuck if necessary. In fact, almost every other culture but ours recognizes the role played by some kind of emotional energy release, or catharsis, in healing.

Approaches that manipulate this kind of energy are almost unanimously rejected by most of Western medicine, with the possible exception of acupuncture, a discipline still looked on with suspicion." – Dr. Candace Pert, PhD, *Molecules of Emotion*

Why Practice Tibetan Shamanic Qigong (Qi Dao)?
By Ricardo B Serrano, R.Ac.

After finishing late this year 2009 my Qi Dao advance studies with Lama Tantrapa Rinpoche in Tigard, Oregon, the following theories on Qigong, and Qi Dao with body, mind and spiritual benefits are my own opinions and experiences I have derived from practicing and coaching this transformative and empowering Tibetan Shamanic Qigong called Qi Dao - *the art of being in the flow with the Dao*.

For thousands of years, Qigong formed the foundation of Oriental Medicine because Qi, universal energy or life force, is the basis of life, therefore, energy awareness offers us the key to health, happiness and longevity. Most styles of Qigong use movements, breathing, meditation and visualization for the purpose of cultivating Qi. They are often taught through *'doing forms,'* or *choreographed movements*, that are to be memorized and repeated on a regular basis.

Tibetan Shamanic Qigong also called Qi Dao goes back to the Shamanic roots of Qigong and encourages its practitioners to stay true to the universality of this energy art. Qi Dao teaches us how to feel the flow of energy, how to be in the flow and simply surrender to that flow. The practice of Qi Dao includes no routines of repetitive movements that are supposed to manipulate or cultivate Qi. Aside from being a *powerful internal martial art* and ultimately dedicated to *self-realization* and *awakening*, it is an energy healing modality facilitating *self-healing*. It teaches us that there is an abundant source of energy within us that we can tap by paying attention to the existing flow of Qi without any judgements. Empowering others to embody such an attitude became the hallmark of Qi Dao coaching.

The use of the *energy ball* and the four universal elements earth, water, air and fire are the hallmarks of Qi Dao to embody and master being in the flow in the six branches of the Qigong tree. The six branches of the Qigong tree that correspond to the historical Qigong branches and comprise the six main applications of Qi Dao are:

- *Daoist Qigong* - Dao Yin - primarily dedicated to wellness and longevity
- *Wushu Qigong* - Internal Martial Art - for self-defense and conflict resolution
- *Tantric Qigong* - Tantra Yoga - for mutual self-realization through enlightened relationships
- *Therapeutic Qigong* - Qigong Therapy - for holistic energy healing and prevention
- *Confucian Qigong* - Mastery Coaching - for manifesting your innermost dreams
- *Buddhist Qigong* - Dream Yoga - for spiritual awakening in the dream called life.

Physical Benefits:
Because of the magic of touch and regular practice of Qi Dao's harmonious culture of movement, the physical discomforts such as shoulder, back and other body pains I used to suffer from are now history together with cardiovascular and immune system energy fields (*Wei Qi*) strengthening results

Psychological Benefits:
Most of the stress-related disorders caused by the six holding patterns with their psychological and emotional states such as Holding Forth (anger), Holding Back (judgemental), Holding In (fear), Holding Out (cynical), Holding Down (depression) and Holding Up (pride) have all been managed and prevented.

Spiritual Benefits:
Because the *energy blockages*, tension and congestion caused by the *six holding patterns* have all been cleared, and balanced through the practice of the *Wushu, Daoist* and *Therapeutic Qigong*, manifesting the dream of enlightened relationship, self-realization and awakening are now possible through the practice of *Buddhist, Tantric* and *Confucianist* Qigong.

Overall Summary:
From the above body, mind and spiritual mentioned benefits in being rooted, grounded and centered derived from the regular practice of the six main branches of Qi Dao, I am grateful that I started and finished my beginner, intermediate and advance Qi Dao practitioner certification program which cover the necessary Qi Dao empowerment and fundamentals in the six branches of Qigong that provide the missing foundational tools to master the art of **being in the flow with the Dao** that is synonymous with becoming **one with the Dao**. For assistance, please view Lama Tantrapa's YouTube Qi Dao videos.

Most importantly, unlike other Qigong styles without spiritual component which are basically stuck to one chakra similar to psychological or emotional states, the practice of Qi Dao is fluidic, malleable and not stuck to one chakra making it possible for the flow of Qi to become freely unimpeded in every one of the chakras, meridians, organs or parts of the body within one's energy field. This free-flowing fluidity and malleability of Qi, a distinct hallmark of Qi Dao, is what makes it work.

"My research has shown me that when emotions are expressed – whichis to say that the biochemicals that are the substrate of emotion are flowing freely – all systems are united and made whole. When emotions are repressed, denied, not allowed to be whatever they may be, our network pathways get blocked, stopping the flow of the vital feel-good, unifying chemicals that run both our biology and our behavior. This, I believe, is the state of unhealed feeling we want so desperately to escape from. Drugs, legal and illegal, are further interrupting the many feedback loops that allow the psychosomatic network to function in a natural, balanced way, and therefore setting up conditions for somatic as well as mental disorders." – Dr. Candace Pert, PhD, *Molecules of Emotion*

13-Posture Tai Chi

When you're "going with the flow," or in a state of *Wu Wei* via the 13-posture Tai Chi, supple as water, strong as the mountain, you maintain inner tranquility in your everyday life by promoting smooth flow of Qi and blood, harmonize, align, unify the body to *embody being in the flow*. Read (8 Trigrams, 5 Elements) *Wuji Qigong for enlightenment*, p. 74; *Vajrasattva Hitting Qigong*, p. 80

The 13 postures are the basic skills that are the foundation of all Tai Chi Chuan skills. Tai Chi 13 Postures are beautiful when performed and every movement is highly practical in its application. It can be practiced for self-healing, fitness, performance, self defence applications or treatment and prevention of physical and mental disorders by channeling Qi for the emission of power (Fa Jin).

13-posture Tai Chi by Master Helen Liang:
1. Embracing Tai Chi Ball - *Tai Chi Bao Qiu*
2. Wild Horse Parts Its Mane
3. White Crane Spreads It's Wings - *Bai He Liang Chi*
4. Brush Knee and Push - *Lou Xi Ao Bu*
5. Playing Lute - *Shou Hui Pi Pa*
6. Roll Back and Squeeze - *Lu Ji Shi*
7. Step Forward to Deflect, Parry and Punch - *Shang Bu Ban Lan Cu*
8. Ward Off, Roll Back, Squeeze, and Push - *Peng Lu Ji An pen*
9. Cloud Hands - *Yun Shou*
10. Single Whip - *Dan Bian*
11. Snake Creeping Down - *Xia Shi*
12. Cross Punch - Shi Zi Chui and and Step Up, Seven Stars - *Shang Bu Qi Xing*
13. Pluck, Split, Elbow, Strike - *Cai Lie Zhou Kao*

The Five steps move the body. The Eight gates control the power. When combined these are the 13 original forms of Tai Chi Chuan. - *Chang San-feng*, View the *13 Tai Chi form by Sifu Ricardo B Serrano*, http://vimeo.com/800183739/d481431f2b

ADDENDUM: Every Disease is the Outcome of Stress

An important fact that has to considered by holistic practitioners of meditation and Qigong is that every disease is the outcome of a specific core emotional stress or conflict that has to be identified and released to heal disease. From the experience and research of doctors (B. Lipton, C. Sabbah and C. Pert), psychologists and others over the past 30 or more years, it has become clear that chronic disease such as cancer is the result of either a period of prolonged, severe stress or sudden, unexpected severe stress. The severity of disease is determined by the intensity or severity of the stress.

The stress hormones that trigger the fight-or-flight reaction caused by persistent stress over the long term pose serious threats to your health which is why you must address your stress.

Elevated levels of stress hormone cortisol lead to inflammatory conditions such as atherosclerosis. Cortisol suppresses the immune system and also lead to flare-ups of existing conditions such as ulcers, asthma, cold sores or eczema. Elevated levels of stress hormone adrenaline elevate both blood pressure and heart rate increasing your risk of heart attack or stroke.

The chemical changes created by stress can alter brain function and trigger anxiety and depression that produce chronic insomnia, obesity and substance abuse; affects cognitive function such as short and long term memory; and reduces sex drive leading to impotence and lower fertility.

Symptoms of persistent stress include anxious or negative thoughts or feelings, loss of concentration, frequent illness, changes in diet or sleep patterns, nervousness, chest pain, irritability, procastination, and feelings of isolation.

While stress produces many negative effects, they are reversible. In fact, stress can be managed and reduced by going with and being in the flow of all things using Omkabah Lightbody Activation, breathing, meditation, Qigong and other natural Oriental healing modalities to cultivate the Three Treasures Jing, Qi and Shen.

According to Qi Dao Master Lama Tantrapa, "Struggling against the flow of a night-dream is a sure way to turn it into a nightmare. Similarly, if you struggle against the flow of your daily life, you single-handedly turn your life into a nightmare. Going against the flow of things only exhausts your energy, takes a toll on your health, and wastes your time. As soon as you realize that life's challenges can be perceived as learning opportunities rather than problems, you will become less tense or "stressed-out" and find yourself in the flow of life. Being in the flow will empower you to live your dreams."

> "It's not stress that kills us, it is our reaction to it." -- Hans Seyle

Our lives are filled with stress reflected by our mental attitude and emotional experience. Because of our own ignorance, we look for love, happiness, peace, joy and contentment outside where they are not. The meditation and Qigong techniques covered in this book are simple and direct means to experience within you an ocean of love, peace, joy, happiness and well-being in a continuous basis.

However, I believe, based on my research and experience, that the reality of our life is not what is happening to us physically but rather what is happening to us emotionally, of which we are not fully aware. It is the core issue, the underlying emotional story, that we are unconsciously telling ourselves in the background that determines our reactions and shows up in our conscious life experience – emotionally, mentally and physically.

Dr. Nelie Johnson's article *You Hold the Keys to Your Healing* lists the 5 Steps that support healing of major diseases:

1. Adjust your view of disease as much as possible. Think of your body "talking" to you, letting you know that it is responding to a core emotional stress or conflict, and is helping you by storing the stress energy in the physical body, so that you live well for as long as possible.

2. Be curious about your core issue (the underlying emotional story) and begin to be aware of the situations that bother or upset you the most. In other words, notice what pushes your buttons the most. Notice, too, when you go flat, get down or sad. Get to know yourself.

3. When your buttons get pushed, rather than push back with anger and irritation, ask yourself, "What is really getting to me? What is my anger? What are my deeper feelings and inner dialogue about this?" Getting upset is an opportunity to get to know yourself.

4. Begin a journal of your experiences and insights.

5. Get support to help you uncover key aspects of your emotional story. Participate in a workshop or arrange private sessions. Most of us need outside help, for we are blind to what is unconscious in us.

"We are sick because we are not aware. Awareness is the key to healing." – Anonymous

You heal the disease when you clear the cause by identifying and releasing the associated pattern of stress. When you clear stress energy, you pull the plug on disease and it has no reason for being. The body can heal itself when there is no emotional block in the way, including your own fears. However, until you clear the stress pattern, disease continues and you need the support of medical treatment and other therapies. Be sure to work closely with your doctors and continue medical treatments for as long as they are needed.

The question to ask yourself is not only "what can this therapy or treatment do for me?" but also "what can I do for myself?" and "what do I need to know about myself and how I live my life and how I am reacting unconsciously?"

When you go after the root cause of disease or "dis-ease" you open up possibilities of deep healing. The rewards you might experience are:
- unburdening yourself of emotional distress, limiting beliefs or a physical condition
- finding freshness, energy and vitality in your life
- creating your life in the moment rather than reacting to an unconscious program and
- replaying the past experiencing greater ease, calmness and sense of well-being

Life experience can manifest as disease or illness. When you bring awareness to the emotional root cause – to the stress pattern and the associated thoughts and beliefs – you empower yourself to heal your life so you may heal physically.

Whether you have recurrent migraine headaches, fibromyalgia, a weight issue, arthritis, a cancer or an unwanted pattern in your life, it is possible to heal.

Whatever the diagnosis, you do not have to expect the worst. There are solutions. "You hold the keys to your healing."
Source: You Hold the Keys to Your Healing by Dr. Nelie Johnson, MD www.awarenessheals.ca

NOTE: The supplementary book Return to Oneness with Spirit has chapters that list proven energy-based strategies such as the Five Agreements, Pan Gu Shen Gong, Qi- healing, Hara (Lower Dantian) breathing, being in the present, Chinese tonic herbs, ear acupuncture, Emotional Freedom Technique (EFT), and EFT Qi-healers Method that support healing of major diseases caused by prolonged emotional stress. Intranasal light therapy is integrated with Qigong to unblock the Qi channels restoring homeostasis.

Study Finds That Intranasal Light Therapy Reduces High Blood Pressure and Cholesterol

In a rigorous study recently published in the International Journal of Photoenergy, researchers found that intranasal low-intensity laser therapy regulates the factors that affect vascular diseases such as high blood pressure and cholesterol. This technology is often known as Intranasal Light Therapy, a technology made available by Vielight of Toronto, Canada.

According to the study leader, Professor Timon Liu of South China Normal University in Guangzhou, China: "Intranasal low-intensity laser therapy has been applied to treat hyperlipidemia, the blood-stasis syndrome of coronary heart disease, myocardial infarction, and brain disease such as insomnia, intractable headache, Alzheimer's disease, Parkinson's disease, post-stroke depression, pain in the head or face, migraine, cerebral thrombosis, diabetic peripheral neuropathy, cerebral infarction, acute ischemic cerebrovascular disease, brain lesion, schizophrenia, cerebral palsy, and mild cognitive impairment."

According to scientific research, intranasal light therapy, stimulates the mitochondria to produce more ATP, and triggers the release of nitric oxide (NO), a powerful cell signaler and activator. NO sends "blood flow signals" that relax arterial walls, dilate the blood vessels, and improve the flow of blood and oxygen everywhere in your body. The results of this study further establishes intranasal light therapy as a credible, non-drug treatment to improve conditions of high blood pressure and cholesterol, which would help to reduce the risk of heart attacks and strokes.

Researchers at South China Normal University worked with the medical practitioners at the Shanghai Pudong District Hospital to investigate the effect of intranasal laser therapy on 90 patients with coronary heart disease. They conducted the study over a period of three months in 2008 under double-blind, placebo-controlled conditions; criteria that help to define a rigorous study. The research examined the changes in key factors that affect blood pressure and cholesterol profile. High blood pressure is a condition that increases the risk of heart attack. It is affected by the "thickness" and flow quality of blood; the factors that contribute to it are blood, plasma and redox viscosity, red blood cell aggregation, and red blood cell concentration. Results show that intranasal light therapy significantly reduces these factors.
The wrong types of fat in the blood can cause the formation of plaques in the blood vessels, increasing the risk of blockage that lead to heart attacks. The combination of plaques with high blood pressure also makes a deadly risk recipe for stroke.
Blood lipid, total cholesterol, triglycerides, high and low density lipoprotein (HDL and LDL) and apolipoprotein are related factors. Results show that intranasal light therapy significantly improves this profile, which would then reduce the risk of a fatal outcome.
The therapy not only reduces LDL (often labelled as the bad cholesterol), it also increases HDL (the good cholesterol). The South China study explains that the therapy influences this and the other phenomena by stimulating the body to restore homeostasis. The healthy person would be in homeostasis, a state when the systems in the body are perfectly balanced. See TCM and sexual dysfunction, p.102

Whole Disease Approach

Dr. Bruce Lipton, cell biologist, researcher, former medical professor:

The medical model that places genes in control of biology is incorrect. Genes provide a blueprint only.

Proteins in the cell, in response to environmental factors, determine which genes are activated.

Environmental signals adjust gene expression so that the individual can adapt and survive maximally in any given situation.

What is Disease? A Wholistic View – it's physical, mental, emotional and spiritual aspects, and each aspect is inter-related:

Disease does have a meaning
Disease represents an automatic biological response of the brain to contain stress Energy. Disease is the expression or outcome of an unresolved emotional/mental trauma or conflict. Brain's primary biological function = to ensure survival
Disease = survival response of the brain.

Dr. Claude Sabbah:
"For healing to occur, it is necessary, and sufficient, to resolve the conflict deep within oneself."
"The root cause of disease is the intimate conflicts of daily life."

Really getting what disease is leads to strategies for healing, not only disease management.

Recognized that it was essential
- To make patient aware of his emotional story
- To make patient aware that the appearance of the disease in his life was the natural outcome of his life story
- To support the patient to deal with fear
- To make the patient the key player in his / her own healing process

His approach provides a modality to manage fear and empower patients to contribute maximally to their own healing.

Quotations from book Molecules of Emotion
by Dr. Candace Pert, PhD

"Western medicine may say "it is all in your head." The paradigm has got to shift. Even if it was entirely mental, thinking it's all in your head shows no awareness of the new research, suggesting the consciousness is a body-mind wide phenomenon." – Dr. Candace Pert

The mind is not just in the brain – it is also in the body. The vehicle that the mind and body use to communicate with each other is the chemistry of emotion. The chemicals in question are molecules, short chains of amino acids called peptides and receptors, that she believes to be the "biochemical correlate of emotion." The peptides can be found in your brain, but also in your stomach, your muscles, your glands and all your major organs, sending messages back and forth. After decades of research, Dr. Pert is finally able to make clear how emotion creates the bridge between mind and body.

Dr. Pert's striking conclusion that it is our emotions and their biological components that establish the crucial link between mind and body does not, however, serve to repudiate modern medicine's gains; rather, her findings complement existing techniques by offering a new scientific understanding of the power of our minds and our feelings to affect our health and well-being.

Dr. Pert explains that perception and awareness play a vital part in health and longevity. She is able to explain how her research bridges the mind and body gap that is sadly prevalent in modern traditional medicine. Her views on mind-body cellular communication mesh well with the concepts of energy held by many alternative therapies, and she is now, not surprisingly, a popular lecturer on the wellness circuit. Her book describes an eight-part program for a healthy lifestyle, and she has appended an extensive list of alternative medicine resources. For all of those who have sought out complementary medicine, this book will confirm what you have long suspected: that alternative approaches to health do work. Dr. Pert explains why.

The scientific basis of the components of the molecules of emotion has basically two parts: The receptors that receive the smaller molecule, kind of into themselves on the surfaces of self. The other half is the ligand, the small molecule that binds to the receptors. These smaller molecules can be drugs, hormones, or other chemicals – chemicals made from within, many of which are peptides in their structure. These are all over, not just the brain but different parts of the body, including the heart and the vessels around the heart.

Do we treat physical conditions from an emotional point of view or vice versa? Dr. Pert says, "I honestly cannot differentiate the physical from the mental, vice versa. The answer is you simultaneously do both, because they're flip sides of the same thing... I think a key word is balance, but I do feel that the meditation if possible twice a day in some kind of ritualized and not free-form form could be the cornerstone of a fitness program, along with exercise, which many studies have shown is the critical anti-aging variable in all kinds of animals and human beings." www.candacepert.com

70-80% of people are magnesium deficient. Magnesium deficiency is a public health crisis of epic proportions. Mitochondria are the powerhouses of cells, producing ATP energy in the Krebs cycle. – Dr. Carolyn Dean, MD, ND

Coenzyme Q10 (CoQ10), the essential nutrient by Ricardo B Serrano, R.Ac.

CoQ10 is key to our heart health. It's crucial to protecting your mitochondria. This super nutrient is key to delaying or Preventing mitochondrial depletion. A nutrient pyroroloquinoline quinone (PQQ) increases the number of mitochondria.

CoQ10's power begins with its antioxidant abilities, which protect your mitochondria against free radical damage. This stops them aging and dying. But more than this, CoQ10 is a high-octane fuel your mitochondria need to produce the energy they run on. I recommend that everyone take 30 mg of CoQ10 daily. If you're over 60, double that to 60 mg. But if you're suffering from a chronic condition, increase the dose to at least 100 mg a day. And make sure it's the ubiquinol form of CoQ10, which is the most potent.

Magnesium (glycinate) is also required by mitochondria to generate ATP. CoQ10 (ubiquinol) with magnesium glycinate supplementation is best integrated with intranasal light therapy for healing chronic diseases such as depression, fatigue, diabetes, hypertension, migraines, PMS, insomnia, arthritis, stroke, osteoporosis, asthma, dementia and cancer. Mitochondrial dysfunction is the root cause of chronic diseases. See Intranasal light therapy, page 98

Glossary of Scientific Terms

Amino acids Amino acids are organic compounds that are the building blocks of proteins and the smaller peptides. Proteins are large, naturally occurring polypeptides.

Cytokine/chemokine (interleukin, lymphokine) An effort was made to systematize the nomenclature, and, as the identification of these potent biological mediators remains a subject of intense research, this process continues. For example, for a while, the name interleukin was used to emphasize the "interleukocyte" nature of the information flow, and a "lymphokine" was the hormonal secretion of a lymphocyte. However, almost as soon as these concepts were established and set forth, it became clear that such communication neither originated solely in lymphocytes nor was confined to lymphocytes. The more general term of "cytokine" emphasizes that some cytokines cause "chemotaxis." See also leukocyte.

Chemotaxis The ability of cells, including bacteria and other unicellular organisms, to move toward a chemical stimulus. Because cells will move toward (chemotax) higher concentrations of the stimulus, its controlled release enables it to serve as a chemotactic meditator, recruiting cells to specific sites in the body where and when they are needed.

Endogenous Originating or produced within an organism, a tissue, or a cell. The opposite of exogenous.

GABA receptors are a class of receptors that respond to the neurotransmitter gamma-aminobutyric acid (GABA), the chief inhibitory neurotransmitter in the vertebrae central nervous system. There are two classes of GABA receptors, GABAa known as ionotropic receptors, and GABAb receptors known as metabotropic receptors.

Leukocyte A white blood cell, a generic term for the lymphocytes, monocytes, and other cells of the immune and host-defense system.

Ligand From the Latin ligare, "that which binds" (same root as religion). Any of a variety of small molecules that specifically bind to a cellular receptor and in so doing convey an informational message to the cell.

Molecule The smallest particle into which an element or a compound can be divided without changing its chemical and physical properties. A molecule is composed of several, perhaps many atoms.

Neuron Any of the impulse-conducting cells that constitute the brain, spinal column, and nerves, consisting of a nucleated cell body with one or more dendrites and a single axon. Also called nerve cell. Synapse The junction across which a nerve impulse passes from an axon terminal to a neuron, a muscle cell, or a gland cell. **Neuropeptide** Any of the nearly 100 small peptide informational substances initially described as neuronal secretions. More recent observations that lymphocytes and monocytes both secrete and respond to neuropeptides has, of course, rendered this term somewhat inaccurate, and immunologists favor terms like cytokine or chemokine, but neuroscientists still commonly refer to neuropeptides.

Neurotransmitter A chemical substance, such as acetylcholine or dopamine, that transmits nerve impulses across a synapse. Peptide Any of various natural or synthetic compounds containing two or more amino acids linked by the carboxyl group of one amino acid and the amino group of another. By definition, polypeptides are the larger peptides, usually those with in excess of 100 amino acids. But they are smaller than the proteins, which may have 200 or more amino acids as well as other attached molecules, such as sugars or lipids.

Protein A complex organic macromolecule that is composed of one or more chains of amino acids. Proteins are fundamental components of all living cells and include many substances, such as enzymes, hormones, and antibodies, that are necessary for the proper functioning of the organism.

PNI Psychoneuroimmunology. A term coined in the early eighties to emphasize and promote research that is interdisciplinary in focus and attempts to understand how mental (psychological) function affects immunological activities mediated via traditional neuronal connections. Neuroimmunomodulation is another variant term in which psyche is subsumed (implied) within "neuro." Receptor A molecule, typically a protein or group of proteins, anchored in the outer cell membrane with a site accessible to the outside environment that binds with ligands such as hormones, antigens, drugs, peptides, or neurotransmitters – all those ligands been referred to as "informational substances." The receptor is the key player in the communication network of the bodymind, as it is only when the receptor is occupied by the ligand that the information encoded in the informational substances can be received. It is also at the receptor that the earliest informational processing occurs, as the actual signal the receptor transduces to the cell can be modulated by the action of other receptors and their ligands, the physiology of the cell, and even past events and memories of them.

TCM and sexual dysfunction

Strengthening Jing and the Life-Gate are often the first approach when working with sexual dysfunction and general health problems, according to Traditional Chinese medicine (TCM).

Weakness of Life-Gate Fire-The Gate of Life or Ming men is (located on the middle of the lower back) is an essential part of traditional Chinese physiology. Called the "Gate of Life," it holds the Yin and Yang of the body from which all substances and functions develop. Along with the Yin-Yang theory, one of the most fundamental principles in Chinese medicine is that of the "Three Treasures." The Three Treasures consist of jing (essence/potential energy), qi (energy/function), and shen (spirit or spirits). In terms of understanding the Ming Men the concepts of jing and qi are primary. Original Qi is stored in an energetic center called Ming Men. The relationship between the Kidney organ-system and Ming Men is defined by the relationship between the elements of Water and Fire, or Kidney and Heart as explained above. Strengthening Jing and the Life-Gate are often the first approach when working with ED/Impotency and general health problems.

Erectile dysfunction (ED)/Impotence
Seminal discharge, white/cold
Dizziness/vertigo
Tinnitus
Pale complexion,
Cold extremities
Listlessness of spirit
Weak aching lower back and legs
Frequent urination
Pale Tongue with white coating
Deep thready pulse
Qi Gong has specific movements to strengthen the Gate of Life.

Acupuncture, tonic herbs, Qigong and massage can help to balance the Qi flow and rehabilitate individuals with sexual dysfunction and general health problems. Intranasal light therapy is an important adjunct to rebuild Jing and Qi to heal sexual dysfunction and other chronic diseases.

American ginseng

Benefits of american ginseng: improving memory, increasing vitality, extending endurance, fighting fatigue, resisting disease, boosting of the immune system, balancing metabolism, treating sleep disorders and overcoming insomnia, regulator of blood sugar levels, cholesterol levels, and blood pressure, as a general tonic to aid in both mental and physical activity. Best when taken in tea form with tongkat ali and horny goat weed (epimedium) taken in capsule form.

Tongkat Ali

Eurycoma longifolia is a shrub native to Southeast Asia. It goes by many names: in Indonesia it is known as pasak bumi; in Malaysia, tongkat ali (ali's walking stick); and Thailand, cay ba binh. Tongkat ali and longjack are the most commonly used names for the herb in the Western world.

Tongkat Ali is probably best known for enhancing sexual vitality, but this remarkable herb provides broad adaptogenic and balancing properties for both women and men. The list of traditional uses is long and includes promoting general vitality with aging, invigorating sexual vitality, enhancing strength, muscle mass and bone mass, supporting balanced mood, strengthening stress tolerance, and supporting energy and general health.

Side effects: Though reports of side effects are mild and few, the potential side effects include nausea and upset stomach; therefore, tongkat ali should be taken with food. Because tongkat ali is an energizing adaptogen, it should be used with caution by individuals with sleep issues or who are overcoming health adversity. Like many herbs, tongkat ali has mild blood thinning properties; if you are taking prescription blood thinners, consult your healthcare provider before taking tongkat ali.

Horny Goat Weed

Epimedium (horny goat weed) is a low-growing perennial plant native to China, Japan, and Korea. There are 52 species of epimedium offering similar properties; Epimedium grandiflorum is a the most common species found in supplements in the Western world.

In the Western world, epimedium is primarily known for its benefits to sexual vitality, but in China, epimedium is a highly revered herb that has been used for a variety of purposes for at least 2,000 years.

In Traditional Chinese Medicine (TCM), epimedium was used to restore vitality and strengthen the body, with sexual performance being one benefit of that larger goal. Strengthening the body included supporting healthy muscle and bone mass, strengthening the heart and cardiovascular system, promoting joint health, enhancing energy, and supporting optimal immune functions and healthy aging.

Side effects: Possible mild side effects include sleep disturbances and nervousness. Because epimedium is an energizing adaptogen, it should be used with caution by individuals with sleep issues or who are overcoming health adversity. Like many herbs, epimedium has mild blood thinning properties; if you are taking prescription blood thinners, consult your healthcare provider before taking epimedium.

NOTE: The herbal formulas become more potent when combined with NO (nitric oxide boosters) like L-Citrulline, beet root, gingko biloba with intranasal light therapy. Omega 3 fish oil 1000 mg., Vitamin E 200 IU a can be taken a day, but not taken with statin drugs and niacin that are blood thinners. Please consult a health professional for an individual session with acupuncture, tonic herbs, Qigong and acupressure massage. Thank you!

Avoid high fat fried food that clog your arteries. *"He who takes medicine yet neglects his diet, wastes the skills of the physician."* - Chinese proverb

With thanks and acknowledgements to the following authors who have contributed greatly with their inspiring articles toward the research of this book

Dr. Nelie Johnson, MD is a family physician and facilitator for healing - inspiring and guiding people to tap into their own healing potential. She is a contributing author to a bestselling book and provides seminars, workshops, and private consultations. www.awarenessheals.ca

Dr. Candace Pert, PhD is an internationally recognized pharmacologist who has published over 300 scientific articles on peptides and their receptors and the role of these neuropeptides in the immune system. Her earliest work as a researcher involved the discovery of opiate receptors and the actions of receptors. She has an international reputation in the field of receptor pharmacology and chemical neuroanatomy. Dr. Pert has lectured worldwide on these and other subjects, including her theories on emotions and mind-body communication. Her popular book, *"Molecules of Emotion, Why You Feel the Way You Feel,"* (Scribner, September 1997) expounds on her research and theories. She was featured in "Washingtonian" magazine (Dec. 2001) as one of Washington's fifty "Best and Brightest" individuals. www.candacepert.com

Master Tao Huang is a native Taoist from China. He was initiated by his spiritual father, Lao Zi, to present Taoist Inner Alchemy to the west. Tao has a B.A. in Psychology and is an Abbot at Ascending Hall, a Taoist Temple. Master Huang has published three books on Taoism. He is the author of a number of books, including Spiritual Anatomy: Your Journey Through Nehemiah's Dream Gates, Laoism: The Complete Teachings of Lao Zi (Lao Tzu), The Secrets of the Tao Te Ching, and Door to All Wonders: Application of the Tao Te Ching. He is currently working on a new book, Angelic Wings, which deals with the divine romance of yin and yang. He was also ordained into the 26th lineage of the Dragon Gate School in China.

Master Choa Kok Sui is the Founder and Originator of the Pranic Healing and Arhatic Yoga System, as well as the internationally acclaimed author of the book, Miracles Through Pranic Healing (3rd Edition). Originally published in 1987 as The Ancient Science and Art of Pranic Healing, Master Choa conceptualized a fresh and far deeper understanding of energy healing, using the readily available source of all life - Prana, called Pranic Energy or Vital Life Force. He is Ricardo B Serrano's Pranic Healing and Arhatic Yoga teacher.

This book has been translated into over 27 languages, and is distributed in more than 40 countries. A prolific author, other books written by Master Choa Kok Sui include: Pranic Psychotherapy (1990), Advanced Pranic Healing (1992), Pranic Crystal Healing (1996), Psychic Self Defense for Home and Office (1999), and Meditations for Soul Realization (2000). www.pranichealing.com

Michael Winn is the Founder and Director of Healing Tao University summer retreat program (now at Heavenly Mountain in North Carolina's Blue Ridge Mtns, near Asheville). The largest Tao arts program in the west. He is Ricardo B Serrano's teacher of Primordial Wuji Qigong and Taoist inner alchemy. www.healingtaousa.com

Lama Tantrapa is the 27th holder of the lineage of Qi Dao that has been fostered in his clan since 1224 AD. He has over 30 years of experience in Qi Dao and other internal martial arts. He authored the book and DVD entitled "*Qi Dao - Tibetan Shamanic Qigong: The Art of Being in the Flow.*"

Dr. Carolyn Dean, MD, ND, author of The Magnesium Miracle, Discover the missing link to total health (second edition).

Dr Lew Lim, ND, inventor of Vielight intranasal light therapy devices: 633 Red (LED) and 655 Prime (low-level laser) for systemic healing with 810 infrared for brain stimulation.

Dr. Master Zhi Gang Sha, a bestselling author, Qigong master and a Tao grandmaster. He is Ricardo B Serrano's teacher of Da Bei Zhou compassion mantra and Tao Healing Hands. He is instrumental in Ricardo's experiencing oneness with the Tao.

Ricardo B Serrano, R.Ac.

Ricardo B. Serrano, R.Ac., a registered acupuncturist, author of Meditation and Qigong Mastery book with Omkabah Heart Lightbody Activation, Serpent of Light Omkabah, and Maitreya (Shiva)

Shen Gong Procedure videos and other related meditation and healing books, Qi-healer and certified Qigong teacher/ founder of Maitreya (Shiva) Shen Gong and integrative Enlightenment Qigong. He has been trained by Pan Gu Shen Gong Master Ou Wen Wei, Wuji Qigong Master Michael Winn, Sheng Zhen Qigong Master Li Jun Feng, Master Pranic Healer Choa Kok Sui, Zhan Zhuang Qigong Tai Chi Master Helen Liang, Merkaba Master Alton Kamadon, Qi Dao Master Lama Somananda Tantrapa, Toltec Master don Miguel Ruiz, Sri Vidya teacher Raja Choudhury, Tao Grandmaster Zhi Gang Sha (left photo), Buteyko teacher Patrick McKeown and other meditation, herbal, acupuncture teachers.

Praying by Mantra chanting and Tao Healing Hands

Praying to Tao (God) and Kuan Yin with 87 Buddhas for healing and transformation.

He has been practicing herbology, Qi-healing (Qigong with acupuncture) for over 40 years. He specializes in

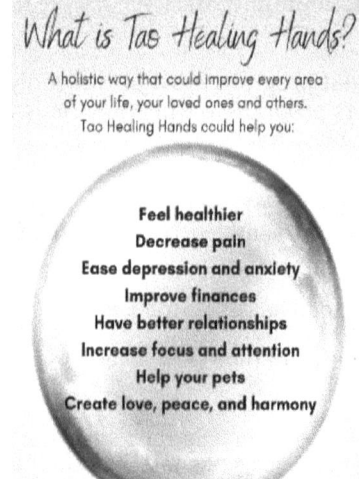

stress and pain management, sexual dysfunction, cancer and other chronic diseases, and alcohol and drug rehabilitation through natural healing alternative modalities such as counselling, meditation, nutrition, exercise, Qigong, intranasal light therapy, acupuncture, EFT, herbs, acupressure and Tao Healing Hands.

He continues to educate his clients and everyone worldwide through his meditation and Qigong workshops, books and videos, and holistic websites: holisticwebs.com, qiwithoutborders.org, qigonghealer.com, freedomhealthrecovery.com, qigongmastery.ca, acutcmdetox.com, keystohealing.ca quantumnaturalhealth.com, and innerway.ca.

His seven other books: *The Cure and Cause of Cancer, Return to Oneness with Shiva, Oneness with Shiva, Return to Oneness with Spirit through Pan Gu Shen Gong, Keys to Healing and Self-Mastery according to the Hathors, Meditation and Qigong Mastery, Six healing Qigong sounds with Mantras.*

www.ingramcontent.com/pod-product-compliance
Lightning Source LLC
Chambersburg PA
CBHW080251170426
43192CB00014BA/2646